The Journey

Toward Recovery

Youth with Brain Injury

A House Between Homes
Youth in the Foster Care System

A Different Way of Seeing
Youth with Visual Impairments and Blindness

The Ocean Inside
Youth Who Are Deaf and Hard of Hearing

My Name Is Not Slow
Youth with Mental Retardation

Chained
Youth with Chronic Illness

Runaway Train
Youth with Emotional Disturbance

Stuck on Fast Forward
Youth with Attention-Deficit/Hyperactivity Disorder

Why Can't I Learn Like Everyone Else?
Youth with Learning Disabilities

Finding My Voice
Youth with Speech Impairment

Somebody Hear Me Crying
Youth in Protective Services

Guaranteed Rights
The Legislation That Protects Youth with Special Needs

The Journey Toward Recovery
Youth with Brain Injury

Breaking Down Barriers
Youth with Physical Challenges

On the Edge of Disaster
Youth in the Juvenile Court System

The Hidden Child
Youth with Autism

The Journey Toward Recovery

Youth with Brain Injury

BY JOAN ESHERICK

MASON CREST PUBLISHERS

Mason Crest Publishers Inc.
370 Reed Road, Broomall, Pennsylvania 19008
(866) MCP-BOOK (toll free)
www.masoncrest.com

First edition, 2004
13 12 11 10 09 08 07 06 05   10 9 8 7 6 5 4 3 2

Library of Congress Cataloging-in-Publication Data:

Esherick, Joan.
The journey toward recovery: youth with brain injury / by Joan Esherick.
v. cm.—(Youth with special needs)
Includes bibliographical references and index.
Contents: Gone—Confusion—Frustration and bitterness—One day at a time—Therapy—Running into reality—Hard work and determination—Hidden gifts.
1. Brain-damaged children—Rehabilitation—Juvenile literature. [1. Brain damage. 2. People with physical disabilities.}I.Title. II. Series.
RJ496.B7E83 2004
618.92'8—dc22. 2003018640
ISBN 1-59084-734-2
1-59084-727-X (series)

Design by Harding House Publishing Service.
www.hardinghousepages.com
Composition by Bytheway Publishing Services, Inc., Binghamton, New York.
Cover art by Keith Rosco.
Cover design by Benjamin Stewart.
Produced by Harding House Publishing Service, Vestal, New York.
Printed in the Hashemite Kingdom of Jordan.

Picture credits: Autumn Libal: p. 23; Benjamin Stewart: pp. 53, 57, 84, 108; Corbis: pp. 37, 40, 41, 42, 89; Life Art: pp. 18, 25, 38, 74, 115; Patricia Therrien: pp. 52, 58, 69, 70, 90, 98, 106, 107; PhotoDisc: pp. 19, 21, 26, 27, 28, 72, 73, 86; Research Foundation/Camp Abilities: pp. 55, 117.

CONTENTS

A child with special needs is not defined by his disability.
It is just one part of who he is.

INTRODUCTION

Each child is unique and wonderful. And some children have differences we call special needs. Special needs can mean many things. Sometimes children will learn differently, or hear with an aid, or read with Braille. A young person may have a hard time communicating or paying attention. A child can be born with a special need, or acquire it by an accident or through a health condition. Sometimes a child will be developing in a typical manner and then become delayed in that development. But whatever problems a child may have with her learning, emotions, behavior, or physical body, she is always a person first. She is not defined by her disability; instead, the disability is just one part of who she is.

Inclusion means that young people with and without special needs are together in the same settings. They learn together in school; they play together in their communities; they all have the same opportunities to belong. Children learn so much from each other. A child with a hearing impairment, for example, can teach another child a new way to communicate using sign language. Someone else who has a physical disability affecting his legs can show his friends how to play wheelchair basketball. Children with and without special needs can teach each other how to appreciate and celebrate their differences. They can also help each other discover how people are more alike than they are different. Understanding and appreciating how we all have similar needs helps us learn empathy and sensitivity.

In this series, you will read about young people with special needs from the unique perspectives of children and adolescents who are experiencing the disability firsthand. Of course, not all children with a particular disability are the same as the characters in the stories. But the stories demonstrate at an emotional level how a special need impacts a child, his family, and his friends. The factual material in each chapter will expand your horizons by adding to your knowledge about a particular disability. The series as a whole will help you understand differences better and appreciate how they make us all stronger and better.

—*Cindy Croft*
Educational Consultant

YOUTH WITH SPECIAL NEEDS provides a unique forum for demystifying a wide variety of childhood medical and developmental disabilities. Written to captivate an adolescent audience, the books bring to life the challenges and triumphs experienced by children with common chronic conditions such as hearing loss, mental retardation, physical differences, and speech difficulties. The topics are addressed frankly through a blend of fiction and fact. Students and teachers alike can move beyond the information provided by accessing the resources offered at the end of each text.

This series is particularly important today as the number of children with special needs is on the rise. Over the last two decades, advances in pediatric medical techniques have allowed children who have chronic illnesses and disabilities to live longer, more functional lives. As a result, these children represent an increasingly visible part of North American population in all aspects of daily life. Students are exposed to peers with special needs in their classrooms, through extracurricular activities, and in the community. Often, young people have misperceptions and unanswered questions about a child's disabilities—and more important, his or her *abilities*. Many times, there is no vehicle for talking about these complex issues in a comfortable manner.

This series provides basic information that will leave readers with a deeper understanding of each condition, along with an awareness of some of the associated emotional impacts on affected children, their families, and their peers. It will also encourage further conversation about these issues. Most important, the series promotes a greater comfort for its readers as they live, play, and work side by side with these individuals who have medical and developmental differences—youth with special needs.

—Dr. Lisa Albers, Dr. Carolyn Bridgemohan, Dr. Laurie Glader
Medical Consultants

We're prepared for some of life's changes . . . but other changes take us by surprise—and when they do, we can only perceive them as disasters.
—Sarah Fairview

1

GONE

The sun felt warm on Jerome's bare shoulders as he sat munching on the granola bar he'd just taken from his bike pack. His legs and arms felt crusty with dirt and sweat; his hair dripped with perspiration. He was chilled, but it was a good chill, the kind that comes after your body works really hard, then pauses to rest a while. Granted, the cold, lumpy boulder he reclined on wasn't comfortable, but it provided relief from the constant jarring of the mountain biking he and his best friends, Eric and Tommy, had been doing all morning. It felt good to relax in the sun.

"Yo, Germ," Eric called to Jerome.

Eric was one of only three people who could get away with calling Jerome by his childhood nickname, a name he earned in first grade when he gave the chicken pox to everyone else in his class. That was nearly ten years ago. Now, only Eric, Tommy, and Jerome's kid sister Jenny, who first said "Germ" when she was little because she couldn't say "Jerome," dared to call him that. He wouldn't stand it from anyone else.

Eric slowly sat up from his grassy spot next to the boulder where Jerome rested. "I've been thinkin' a lot about what happened at practice."

"What! You feelin' sorry for the geek now?" Jerome cocked his head in disbelief.

"Well . . . no . . . I don't know. I mean, like, yeah . . . well no . . . I guess it *could've* been funny.

"It *was* funny," Tommy cut in. Blindly loyal to Jerome, Tommy always took Jerome's side no matter which side of right or wrong Jerome found himself on. "Did you see the look on Stevie's face when he plowed into Coach?"

"I guess. But, I don't know," Eric continued. Ignoring Tommy for a minute, he looked up at Jerome, took a deep breath, and exhaled slowly. "It's not like he can help being the way he is." Then he glanced away.

Eric played the conscience of their trio. It had always been that way. They each had a role to play and played it well.

Jerome was a popular, do-no-wrong prankster, unquestioned leader, and athlete extraordinaire—everybody loved him and wanted to be like him. At Northeast High School, being Jerome's friend meant that you'd arrived—a pretty impressive status considering that Jerome was only a junior. But then again, he'd always been ahead of the game. Now, as a starting varsity football player, Jerome's standing in the invisible hierarchy of senior high social life was secure. He reigned supreme.

Tommy, meanwhile, played the consummate groupie. He was Jerome's go-fer and all-around yes-man. Everyone knew he belonged to Jerome's inner circle only because they'd grown up together and their families had been life-long friends. His athletic prowess certainly didn't qualify him; he played third-string football. But bench-warming on Jerome's team was better than not being part of the team at all. He was content with his part.

But Eric was different. Sure, he clowned around with the best of them and was a gifted athlete, but he also cared about the underdog, a concern that had intensified after watching his mother struggle with cancer. She'd won the first skirmish and was cancer free, but her battle changed the way Eric looked at things. Life wasn't a game anymore. Things happened. People got hurt or sick when it wasn't their fault, and sometimes there was nothing anyone could do. His mom's illness taught him that, and he discovered compassion and boldness along the way. Eric was willing to speak up now in ways he'd never risked before—something Jerome found irritating. Still, although he'd never admit it of course, Jerome secretly admired Eric.

"C'mon, guys," Eric confronted his friends. "I mean, tying Stevie's shoelaces to the practice bench while he was sitting there keeping the books?" Eric looked at Jerome questioningly, then dropped his gaze and started pulling the grass next to him. "The kid has enough trouble walking as it is. He coulda gotten hurt, you know. And he was only doing what Coach told him to do."

"We don't need some gimp like him keeping our stats!" Jerome seethed as he sat up on the boulder. "Especially when I'm starting varsity. All I need is for him to screw up the record, which he will, and then my stats go in the toilet. I'm counting on those stats for a scholarship. Besides, a kid like that doesn't belong on *any* football team, let alone ours. We're better off without him."

Jerome's anger surprised Eric, but he persisted. "Look, Germ, Stevie may not be able to walk right, but he's good at math; he's in geometry with me, and he's really smart." Eric paused, then plowed ahead. "He's okay, once you get to know him. He'll do a great job on the . . ."

"Just get off it, man!" Jerome stood up. "What's wrong with you? I was only thinking about the team. I thought if I did some of this stuff, maybe he'd get the hint and just quit. I don't get what the big deal is anyway. Everybody else thought it was funny. Even *Stevie* laughed." Jerome snatched his lunch pack and stormed back to where the bikes were parked by the trail.

"What's up with him?" Eric looked at Tommy. Tommy shrugged. Then, glancing back to where Jerome had just reclined, Eric noticed Jerome's biking helmet.

"Yo! You forgot your lid," Eric called after his retreating friend.

"I don't need it." Jerome shouted over his shoulder as he mounted his bike. "I'm outta here."

Tommy and Eric scrambled to gather their gear, but by the time they reached the bikes their friend was gone. They'd have to ride fast to catch him.

I don't get Eric anymore. Jerome fumed as he pedaled down the mountain. The wide, flat, cinder path made for smooth riding, a nice change of pace from the rocky woods trail they'd covered earlier in the day. Jerome's mind wasn't on the changing trail, though; it was on his changing friend.

Ever since his mom got sick. He can't take a joke. He's always defending people. Man, I just wish the old Eric would come back. The old Eric would've helped me tie Stevie's laces to the bench post! The old Eric would've laughed along with the rest of us. The old Eric wouldn't have apologized or helped the kid up.

But something else was bugging Jerome. He suspected his friend was right.

A sudden rustling ahead startled Jerome out of his daydream. Pumping the brakes, he strained to see what caused the commotion. In an instant, a dog, its leash dragging on the ground, darted out of the shrubs, then stopped dead in the trail.

The next several seconds seemed to pass in slow motion. The confused Labrador looked straight at the oncoming rider. Jerome squeezed hard on the hand brakes, but it was too late. His front wheel collided with the hundred-pound animal; the dog yelped, and Jerome somersaulted over his handlebars.

Tommy said later that he would never forget how his friend flew through the air and collided head-on with the sycamore tree's trunk. Eric said he'd never forget the sickening thud the impact made. But what his friends would never forget, Jerome would never remember. In a brilliant white flash, Jerome's world and life as he knew it was gone.

"Oh man, what do we do?" Tommy yelled to Eric as the two leapt off their still moving bikes and ran toward their injured friend. The dog, who seemed remarkably unhurt, scurried down the trail with only a slight limp.

"Wait. There's a ranger station up ahead about a half mile. You go get a ranger, and I'll stay here with Jerome." Eric commanded.

Tommy started running down the path.

"Tommy! Take your bike, dude! It's faster."

"Oh yeah, right." Tommy turned around, came back for his bicycle, and rode toward the ranger station like a man possessed.

Eric turned his attention to his unconscious friend. Jerome looked like a rag doll carelessly tossed aside by its owner. His forehead swelled with what looked to be a sizeable, bark-smudged goose egg. A small trickle of blood oozed out of the egg's center. But, all-in-all, the teenager didn't look bad—at least not to Eric. Lying flat on his back and unmoving, Jerome looked like the kid Eric had seen on countless sleepovers. Except for the bump on his head and the tree canopy that surrounded them, Jerome could've been sprawled out on his bed at home.

Don't move him, Eric recalled from his health class. If Jerome's neck were injured, moving him could risk greater damage, even **paralysis**. Eric could tell by the rhythmic rising and lowering of Jerome's chest that he was still breathing, but breathing fast.

Eric ran to his bike pack and grabbed the emergency first aid kit his mom made him carry. Running back, he pulled out a gauze compress and knelt by his still unmoving friend. As he began to gently dab the blood trickling out of Jerome's head, Eric started talking.

"Yo, Germ. You okay? Can you hear me?"

Nothing.

"C'mon, man. Wake up!"

No response.

"Jerome! Yo, Jerome! It's me, Eric. C'mon wake up!" Minutes passed. It seemed like hours.

Jerome finally stirred. His eyelids fluttered, then opened, then closed again. He gingerly lifted his left hand to his head.

"Owwwwww."

"Hey, you okay?"

"Head . . . hurts."

"Yeah, don't move. You really wiped out. Tommy went to get help."

"Wwwho? . . . Tommmm . . ." Jerome panted heavily. "Ww . . . what. . . . wwwhere am I?" Jerome's words, barely a whisper, came out in gasps.

"Don't you remember? We were biking. You know, the old railroad bed? That dog came out of nowhere. Man, like, you really scared me."

"Ddd . . . dog? Wwwh . . . what . . . dog?" Jerome moved like he was going to push himself up, then winced.

"No, don't move, man, I mean it. Wait 'til help comes."

"Yeah. . . . 'kay . . . tired."

Jerome seemed to doze again. He was still dozing off and on when the ranger returned with Tommy. He dozed again when paramedics stabilized his neck with a special collar, rolled him onto a backboard, and then strapped him onto a stretcher.

By the time the emergency-room doctors treated him at the hospital, he was a little more awake, but his head spun and he felt like he was going to throw up. His symptoms just wouldn't quit.

When his parents arrived and learned that their son was fine except for a **closed-head injury**, Jerome's head still throbbed. He felt dizzy when doctors described him as having a mild **traumatic brain injury (TBI)**. He threw up when they explained that his brain had bounced against the inside of his skull when he hit the tree, but that the bruising to his brain tissue was minor. Jerome tried to take it all in, but couldn't. His eyes were open, and he could respond to questions, but he just didn't feel "all there."

Phrases like "possible **contusion**," "site of impact," and "no internal bleeding" spun through his head—words he heard but couldn't make sense of. Other words like "***acceleration/deceleration injury***" and "***concussion***" confused him even more. He completely missed the doctors' descriptions of how the skull and other parts of the head work to protect the brain. His didn't understand his parents' jokes about his "hard head" sparing him further injury. He zoned out during the doctors' lectures on helmets and bicycle safety. He even felt lost during their discussion of "admitting him overnight for observation." He just didn't get it. Jerome felt dazed.

Who are all these people? What am I doing here? Why can't I get this fog out of my head? Though conscious enough to notice his mixed-up thinking, he was too tired to care. Had Jerome been clear-headed enough to understand his doctors' words, he would have cared, and cared deeply. But he just fell asleep again.

HOW COMMON ARE HEAD INJURIES?

The Brain Injury Association of America provides the following statistics:

- Every twenty-one seconds one person in the United States sustains a traumatic brain injury (TBI). That amounts to 1.5 million Americans each year.
- Fifty thousand people in the United States die from TBIs each year.
- An estimated 5.3 million Americans (that's more than two percent of the U.S. population) live with disabilities resulting from TBIs.
- Males between the ages of fourteen and twenty-four have the greatest risk of sustaining a traumatic brain injury.

Bicycle accidents are just one common cause of brain injuries.

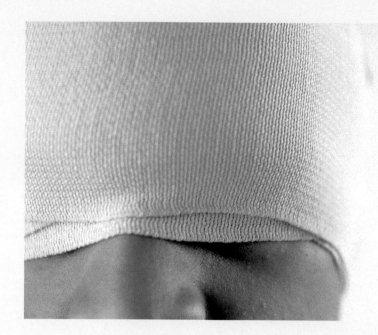

HOW DO BRAIN INJURIES
MOST OFTEN OCCUR?

According to a 1999 study done by the U.S. Centers for Disease Control and Prevention (CDC), the three leading causes of TBIs are motor vehicle accidents, violence, and falls.

The U.S. National Institute of Neurological Disorders and Stroke (NINDS) found that half of all TBIs occurred in transportation accidents involving automobiles, motorcycles, bicycles, and pedestrians.

NINDS also determined that 20 percent of TBIs came from violence involving guns or child abuse.

An estimated three percent of TBIs are related to sports injuries.

Fully half of all TBIs involve alcohol use.

Bicycle accidents cause an estimated 130,000 TBIs each year.

SPORTS: JUST HOW SAFE ARE THEY?

The Brain Injury Association of America provides some interesting sports-related facts:

- More than 750,000 Americans get hurt during recreational sports each year. Of these injuries, 82,000 involve the brain.
- Brain injuries cause more sports-related deaths than any other injury.
- Teenagers suffer more brain injuries than broken bones when skiing, skating, playing ice hockey, and snowboarding.
- Brain injury is the leading cause of death and disability in bicycle crashes.
- Football accounts for 250,000 brain injuries per year, occurring in one out of every three-and-a-half football games. Ten percent of all college football players and 20 percent of high school players sustain brain injuries.
- Five percent of soccer players sustain brain injuries.
- Ninety percent of professional boxers sustain head injuries.
- Brain injuries account for 60 percent of horseback-riding deaths.
- In baseball, the head is involved in more player injuries than any other body part.

THREE WAYS THE BODY PROTECTS THE BRAIN

Some experts liken brain tissue to lumpy custard, tapioca pudding, or thick, pinkish-gray jelly; it is soft and pliable. Because it is so soft, it can be torn, twisted, punctured, or

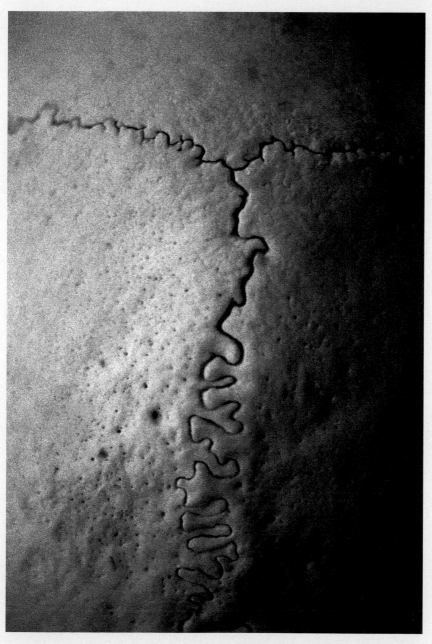

The skull's hard shell protects the brain's delicate tissues.

bruised easily, so it needs protection. Our body protects this delicate organ three ways:

1. The skull: The human skull is the hard bone that surrounds the soft tissues of the brain. The skull is able to absorb, deflect, or diffuse strong blows to the head, preventing injury to the brain.
2. The **dura** mater: The dura mater (also known as the dura) is the strongest of three membranes (known as meninges) that cover brain tissue. Found just inside the skull, this membrane holds air and about a coffee-cup full of fluid around the brain to cushion it.
3. **Cerebrospinal fluid (CSF)**: Also called spinal fluid, this liquid flows in and around the brain, filling any spaces in and around brain matter and allowing the brain to float within the skull. The CSF acts much like an air bag in an automobile, cushioning it from colliding against the skull.

HEAD AND BRAIN INJURIES

Types of Head Injuries

(NOTE: A head injury doesn't always result in a brain injury.)

- Closed-head injury (CHI): an injury to the head that does not penetrate the skull. These might include skull fractures, external bruises, and cuts on the face or scalp.
- **Open-head injury**: an injury that breaks through the skull and dura. These include gunshot wounds, stabbings, or any other injury where the head is opened or pierced by a foreign object. This is sometimes called a **penetrating-head injury**.

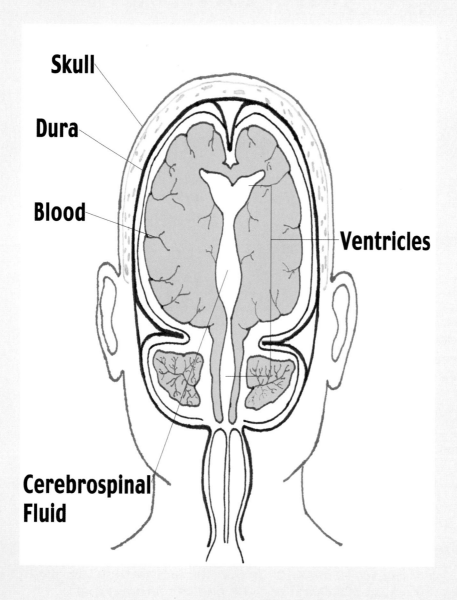

TYPES OF BRAIN INJURIES

- Acquired brain injury: when the brain is damaged by strokes, tumors, lack of oxygen, too much oxygen, poisons, near drowning, degenerative diseases, and other nontraumatic causes.
- Traumatic brain injury (TBI): when the brain is damaged by an external force or a blow to the head, as in automobile accidents, industrial accidents, falls, sports injuries, electric shock, physical abuse, whiplash, weapons injuries, acts of violence, and shaken-baby syndrome. TBIs can result from both closed-head and open-head injuries.
- Congenital brain injury: when the brain is damaged before or during birth (from lack of oxygen, for example).

TYPES OF TBIs

- Acceleration/deceleration injury: An injury where the head moves forward and comes to a sudden stop when it hits a nonmoving object. Though the head stops, the brain moves until it collides with the front of the skull, bruising the brain's frontal lobe.
- Concussion: A minor brain injury that occurs when the brain collides with the skull.
- Contusion: A bruise of a distinct area of brain tissue.
- *Coup/contra-coup* (hit/opposite the hit): An injury that occurs when a moving object hits the head, pressing the skull inward and causing the brain to strike the opposite side of the skull. Bruising occurs at two places: the part of the brain where the head was initially hit and the part of the brain that collided with the opposite side of the skull.
- *Diffuse brain injury*: Tearing and stretching of

A car accident may cause an acceleration/deceleration injury.

microscopic connections throughout the brain; not limited to a specific or confined area.

- **Depressed skull fracture**: When the skull cracks or breaks and pieces of the broken skull press into brain tissue.
- **Edema**: Swelling in the brain, usually due to an accumulation of fluid in brain tissue.
- **Hematoma**: Heavy bleeding in or around the brain. There are three types of hematomas in the head: an **epidural hematoma**, which involves bleeding between the skull and dura mater; a **subdural hematoma**, in which bleeding is confined between the dura mater and the arachnoid membrane; and **intracerebral hematoma**, when the brain itself bleeds.
- **Penetrating skull fracture**: When an object pokes through the skull causing a specific, localized injury to the brain.

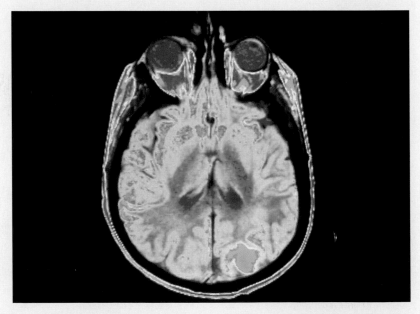

Physicians may use magnetic resonance imaging to locate and diagnose brain injuries.

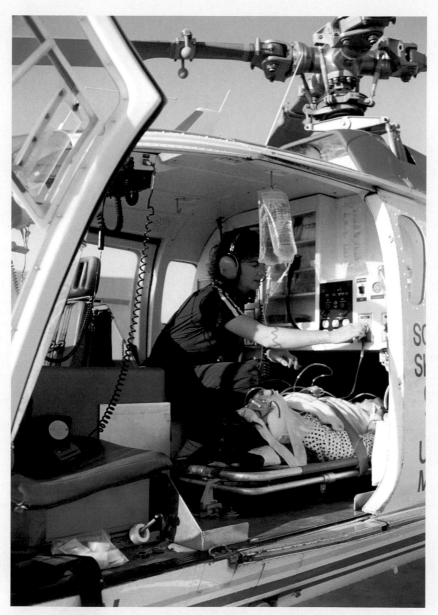

After an accident, victims will be rushed to the hospital for emergency treatment. Immediate medical care is vital after a brain injury has occurred.

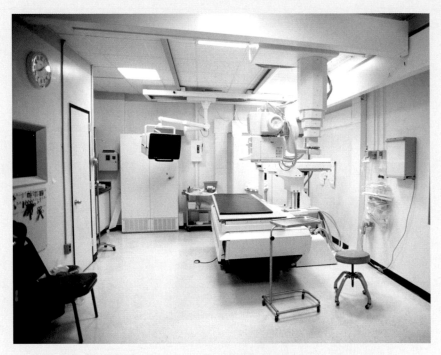

Hospitals are equipped to treat a variety of injuries to the brain.

BRAIN INJURIES ARE NOT ALIKE

Bruising (Bleeding)

When brain tissue collides with the skull, it causes blood vessels to break and bleed into the brain. Severe bleeding (hemorrhaging) is dangerous because the skull cannot expand, so any accumulating blood presses against the soft brain tissue, causing even more damage.

Tearing

When brain tissue is shaken, bounced, or thrown back and forth inside the skull, it can produce microscopic tears all over the brain. These tears, though often invisible in **computed tomography (CT) scans** and **magnetic resonance imaging (MRI)** tests, disrupt the brain's communication signals between cells and can result in problems with thinking, memory, and emotion.

Swelling

As with excessive bleeding, swelling creates a secondary problem because there is no room inside the skull for the brain to expand as it swells. Instead, it pushes inward on surrounding brain tissue, creating pressure that can further damage brain cells.

Even in the thickest fog, the path is still there beneath
our feet . . . even though we can no longer see it.
—Wilma MacDonald

2

CONFUSION

Jerome awoke damp with sweat. His head pounded and his eyes ached as he tried to scan the fuzzy room for clues about where he was and what he was doing there. He started to turn his head but stopped when shards of pain pierced his neck and skull. *Where am I?* his mind screamed in a single moment of clarity. Then clouds of swirling confusion carried him back to his dark slumber.

"He's waking up!" Jerome's mother said almost to herself. Then her tone grew more insistent. "Quick, get the nurse. Your brother's waking up again!"

Jenny scampered into the hall for a nurse.

"Jerome, it's me, Mom," His mother coaxed. "Can you hear me?"

Jerome stirred.

"I'm here, too, son," his father said. "Over here on your left. If you can hear me, squeeze my hand."

Every eye in the room dropped to Jerome's left hand.

"Squeeze my hand, Jerome," his father urged. "You can do it."

Nothing. They waited, eyes riveted on the father–son clasp.

I hear something. What is it? Someone's calling me. They sound so far away. No. . . . I just want to sleep. Let me sleep. Please just let me sleeee. . . .

"What's going on?" Nurse Martin queried as she hurried into the room with Jenny in tow. She checked Jerome's monitors as his mother rushed to tell her.

"He's waking up, again. I'm sure of it. I saw his eyes open, just for a second, but they were open."

The nurse leaned over Jerome's bed and gently raised his eyelid. The pupil shrunk when it came into contact with the light. She checked the other; it reacted normally, too.

"Wake up, Jerome," the nurse insisted as she checked the pulse in his right arm. "Open your eyes."

Jenny nudged her way between the nurse and Jerome's bed rail. Looking between the stainless steel railings, she spoke into Jerome's ear.

"Hey Germie, it's me. You gotta wake up. Please. You promised to take me riding, 'member?"

"Jerome, squeeze my hand," came his father's voice.

"He did it! Did you see?" Jenny squealed.

It was the slightest movement but it was there.

"It could just be an involuntary reflex," the nurse cautioned. "He might still be sleeping. It's not uncommon for someone with a TBI like his to sleep for long periods of time."

"No, it was real. He really did squeeze," Jenny insisted. "I saw it."

"Squeeze my hand again, son," his father repeated. "I'm right here."

Dad? Jenny? Mom? Why is everybody in my room? Oh, yeah, squeeze his hand. I'm supposed to squeeze somebody's hand.

"There! See? He's doing it!"

Jerome could hear Jenny squealing. *Where am I?* He struggled to open his eyes, but each lid felt like it was sewn shut.

"Jerome, wake up!"

With every ounce of strength he had, Jerome willed his eyes open. The white ceiling, the pastel plaid curtain by his bed, the soft green walls, fluorescent lights: it was all wrong. Nothing looked familiar. Everything looked out-of-kilter and distant. The entire scene seemed blurred, like he was looking through eyeglasses smeared with Vaseline. He blinked once. Then again. Then slowly his mother's face came into view.

"Mom?" he whispered.

"Yeah, sweetie. It's me. I love you so much. We've been so worried."

"You really scared us," his father added.

Jerome rolled his eyes slowly toward the direction of the voice. "Dad?"

"I'm here." Mr. Johnson said softly, his voice choked with emotion. "It sure is good to see you awake again."

His father's voice sounded strained. *Why does Dad sound so weird? What happened?* Too many thoughts tumbled through his brain. His head hurt.

"Where . . . am I?" Jerome managed to mumble.

Nurse Martin said, "You're in the hospital, Jerome. You had an accident. Do you remember?"

Accident? What accident?

Jerome barely shook his head, and white flashes went off in his brain. Even the slightest movement caused him blinding pain.

"You were mountain biking with Eric and Tommy yesterday up

on the old railroad-bed trail," his father continued, interrupting the nurse. "They said a dog ran out in front of you, you collided, and then flipped over your handlebars. You hit your head on a tree. Don't you remember?"

"No," the teenager mouthed. He wasn't going to move his head again.

"Eric said the impact knocked you out, but only for a few minutes. Then you seemed to wake up. But you've been sleeping an awful lot since they admitted you to the hospital. Almost eighteen hours now. We thought you were in a **coma**, but the docs assured us that since they could wake you, you were just sleeping. You took quite a bump on the head."

"Well, what have we here?" a strange voice interrupted. It came from the tall man entering the room. Jerome couldn't make out the writing on his lab coat, but guessed he was a doctor. He stared at the stranger approaching his bed, trying to bring him into focus.

"I'm Dr. Wilkerson, Jerome. Do you remember meeting me yesterday?"

"Uh-uh."

"I'm a **neurologist**. Your dad's right; you took a nasty bump to the head. I'm glad to see you're awake again. That's a good sign."

"What's . . . wrong . . . with me?"

"Well, your CT scan was clear, but your MRI shows you have more than just a concussion. You also have a mild contusion on the front part of your brain. When your head hit the tree, it stopped, but your brain, which floats inside your skull, kept moving until it collided with the front part of your skull. When your brain impacted the skull, it bruised, just like your arm or leg gets bruised when you bump into something. The bruise on your brain is called a contusion. It's nothing to be too concerned about. It should clear up on its own in a week or two."

Jerome couldn't understand a word the doctor said, but he played along. "Is that why my head hurts?" he asked weakly.

"Your pain is the result of the head trauma you experienced. We can give you something for the pain while you're here, and I'll write a script for when you go home. You can expect your head to hurt quite a bit for the next few days, but the pain should subside in a few weeks. Still, I think I'd like to keep you here another day to watch your progress. You took quite a spill."

"I just want . . . to . . . sleep." Jerome mumbled, and started to nod off again.

"Should he be sleeping so much?" Jerome's mother asked while her son slept.

"Sure, it's pretty normal," the doctor explained quietly. "He's been through a lot, and the brain is trying to heal, which itself can be an exhausting process. His **Glascow Coma Scale (GCS)** score indicates that he does have a mild to moderate brain injury, and it's not uncommon for people with his degree of brain injury to sleep fourteen, sixteen, even twenty hours a day in the days immediately following their injuries."

"But what about his memory? Why can't he recall what happened to him?"

"He has what's called **post-traumatic amnesia (PTA)**. That's pretty normal following a head injury, too. He'll probably have little, if any, memory of the accident. He may forget the day or two immediately preceding the trauma and will even have little recall of his time here in the hospital. All of that is standard for a patient with a TBI."

"So when can he come home?" Jenny cut in.

"Let's give your big brother another day to rest here. Okay? I'd like to keep an eye on him for another twenty-four hours. Is that all right with you, Jenny?"

Jenny glanced at the big white bed that held her sleeping brother. Then she looked around the room at all the blinking lights and machines. She turned to Dr. Wilkerson, "Okay. I guess. But you'll take care of him, right?"

"You bet!" The doctor assured her.

"And he can come home tomorrow?"

"As soon as it's safe for him to go."

The family felt relieved. They didn't realize that what the doctor defined as "safe" wouldn't seem safe to Jerome at all.

HOW SEVERE IS MY HEAD INJURY?

After a person sustains a head injury, medical personnel will observe his eyes, movement, and talking ability to assess how severe the head injury is. One tool, the Glascow Coma Scale (GCS), rates response levels in three categories:

Response	Cause of response	Score
Opens eyes	spontaneously	4
	prompted by voice	3
	prompted by pain	2
	does not open eyes	1
Moves	prompted by command	6
	pushes away cause of pain	5
	pulls away from pain	4
	flexes in response to pain	3
	becomes rigid in response to pain	2
	does not move	1
Speaks	clearly and without confusion	5
	speaks, but is disoriented and confused	4
	uses inappropriate words and phrases	3
	uses unintelligible sounds	2
	does not speak or attempt to speak	1

Using this scale, trained medical personnel evaluate a person with a head injury, giving him generally a total score (the sum of the three category scores). A total score of 13–15 is considered a mild injury; a score of 9–12 indicates a moderate injury; and a score of 3–8 is considered a severe injury. The lowest possible score is a 3, meaning no response in all three categories.

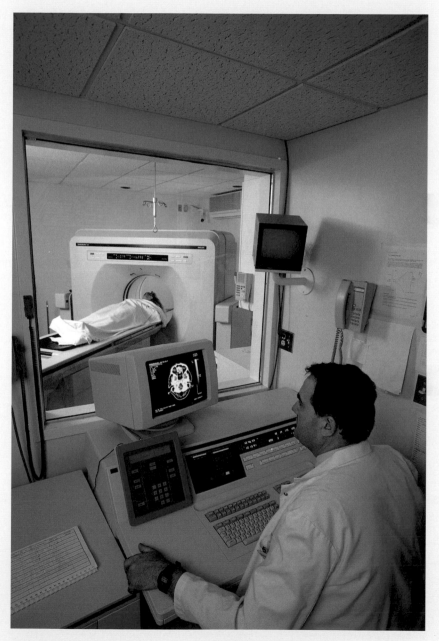

Doctors may use various technologies to assess brain injuries, including CAT scans.

TBI CLASSIFICATION GUIDELINES

There is no universally agreed upon definition for mild, moderate, and severe brain injury. These rankings generally relate to the length of unconsciousness or coma. The International Classification of Diseases ranks TBIs as mild, moderate, or severe using these guidelines:

- Mild TBI: involves less than one hour of coma, momentary loss of consciousness or no loss of consciousness at all.
- Moderate TBI: involves a coma state lasting one to twenty-four hours.
- Severe TBI: involves a coma state lasting twenty-four hours or more.

According to this classification, Jerome experienced a mild TBI.

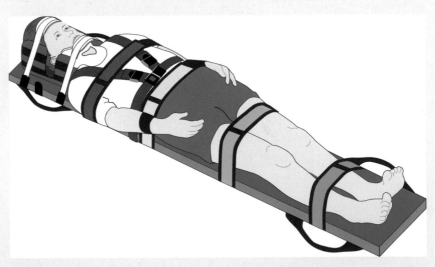

After a head injury, emergency medical personnel will immobilize the victim, in case there has also been injury to the spinal cord.

IS IT SLEEP, UNCONSCIOUSNESS, OR COMA?

When Jenny encouraged Jerome to "wake up," she was right in doing so; Jerome was just sleeping. If he had been in a coma he would not have been able to wake up in response to his sister's encouragement. Medically speaking, a coma is a state of deep unconsciousness caused by an illness or injury. When a person is unconscious, his brain activity is reduced and he is completely unaware of his surroundings. If his unconsciousness is severe enough to keep him from being roused (as with smelling salts), and his unconsciousness lingers, he is said to be in a coma.

Unlike sleep or brief unconsciousness, coma is marked by the three characteristics used in the Glascow Coma Scale:

1. Inability to voluntarily open the eyes.
2. Inability to move in response to simple commands.
3. Inability to talk or communicate in an understandable way.

If a person cannot open his eyes on his own, if he cannot follow simple requests (like "lift your finger" or "squeeze my hand"), and if he cannot respond verbally in an understandable, appropriate way, he is not just asleep; he is, at least, unconscious. If this unconsciousness lasts an hour or more, it is called a coma.

MEDICAL TESTS FOR BRAIN INJURY

Your doctor may ask for special medical tests to determine the exact location and kind of brain injury you sustained. For instance, he may ask for:

- an X-ray of the head and neck to check for bone fractures;
- a CT scan (also known as a CAT scan), which takes a series of cross-sectional picture images and can detect bleeding, swelling, tumors, and other soft tissue injuries;
- an MRI, which uses magnetic fields to show greater detail than X-rays or CT scans. An MRI can detect smaller changes in the brain's tissue;
- a cerebral angiography, which examines blood vessels and the flow of blood in the brain by using special dyes and X-ray techniques; and
- a positron emission tomography (PET) scan, which takes a series of color photographs of a radioactive fluid injected into the brain as it travels through various brain structures.

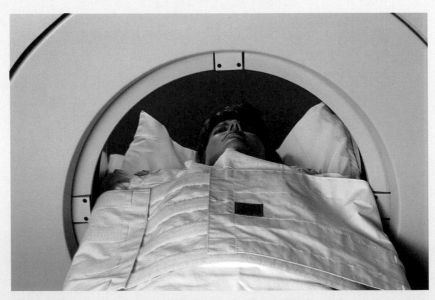

During a CAT scan, the patient lies down and passes through a large doughnut-shaped device.

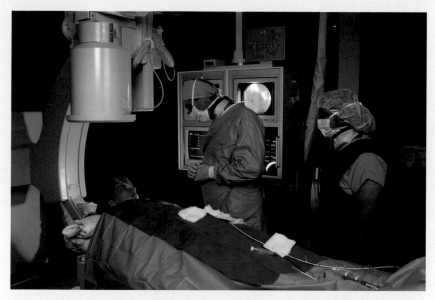

In Phineas Gage's day, doctors could not see what was happening inside Gage's brain—but today's advanced technology allows doctors to look inside the skull.

MOST FAMOUS TBI IN HISTORY

In 1848, railway foreman Phineas Gage and his crew were preparing to lay railroad tracks for the new train that would run near Cavendish, Vermont. To clear the land, twenty-five-year-old Gage used dynamite and other explosive materials. On one occasion, he accidentally set off a charge too soon, and the resulting explosion blew a tamping iron (an iron rod, forty-two inches long and an inch in diameter) through his head. The rod entered Gage's face near his left cheekbone, traveled through his brain and skull, and exited through the top of his head.

Phineas Gage survived despite the fact that most of his left brain was destroyed. After a long stay in the hospital and months of medical care, he returned to work. But he was not the same man. Once friendly and easy-going, the mild-mannered railroad worker became short-tempered, foul-mouthed, and stubborn. His TBI caused a complete personality change for Phineas Gage, and he struggled with behavioral and emotional problems until his death thirteen years later. He was thirty-eight years old when he died.

FAMOUS PEOPLE WITH TBIs

Former President Ronald Reagan's press secretary, James Brady, took a bullet to the head during an assassination attempt on the president in 1980. He survived but lost the use of his left arm and leg and has speech difficulties.

In the 1994 NFL playoffs, Dallas Cowboys' quarterback Troy Aikman suffered a concussion when San Francisco 49er Dennis Brown's knee clipped Aikman's head.

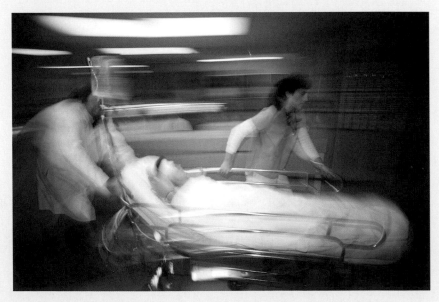

A patient with a brain injury is rushed to surgery.

During the same playoffs, Kansas City Chiefs' quarterback Joe Montana suffered a concussion when his head landed hard on the frozen artificial turf during a tackle.

Detroit Red Wings' defenseman Vladimir Konstantinov and team masseur Sergei Mnatsakanov suffered severe closed head injuries in an automobile accident after celebrating the Red Wings Stanley Cup victory in 1997.

Downhill skier Bill Johnson, who won the Olympic Gold medal in 1984 at the Sarajevo Winter Olympics, sustained a serious brain injury in 2001 when he crashed during a qualifying run for the 2002 Winter Olympics. He spent three weeks in a coma.

Tolstoy said, "Our body is a machine for living." We forget
this fact until a part of the machine breaks down.
—Leah Forster

3

FRUSTRATION AND BITTERNESS

"It must feel good to be home." Jerome's mom enthused as she followed her son into the family room. "Nothing like a few days off!"

"I'm fine, Mom. Really. Will you quit hovering!" Jerome was tired of everyone waiting on him. He was tired of their help. He'd been home from the hospital three days now, and they just wouldn't leave him alone.

"I'm not hovering. I was just picking up these dishes."

Jerome glared at her with his cut-me-a-break look.

"Okay," she admitted. "So I was checking to be sure you got back to the couch okay, too. You've seemed a little unsteady on your feet."

"Just tired, that's all. Quit worrying. I'm *fine*."

"Well, I'm glad the doctor insisted on a few more days of rest," his mother commented as she gathered up the last few dishes in the room. "The last thing you need is to be playing football right now."

Football. Oh, yeah. Right. Football. Jerome thought to himself as he nestled into the sofa. *I've got to get back. The coach won't keep me on varsity if I miss many more practices.*

He leaned forward, ignoring the shooting pain in his head. "How long before I can go back?"

"You mean to football? Oh, the doctor said at least another four weeks. Maybe more. He needs to see you first."

Four weeks! I'll be cut for sure!

45

"Hey, Dude! Hey, Dude's Mom! We're back!" Eric and Tommy interrupted as they sauntered through the family-room door from the deck outside. "We got half cheese, half sausage, just like you ordered."

Cheese? Sausage? What are they talking about? Jerome didn't remember that they'd ordered pizza.

"Sure hope you're hungry, man. We got two." Tommy walked through the family room into the kitchen carrying two flat white boxes.

"Here, let me help you with that," Mrs. Johnson offered, following Tommy into the kitchen. She left her son alone with his best friend in the family room.

"Yeah, right. Whatever. So, how was practice?" Jerome asked, changing the subject.

"You asked us that before we went for pizza," Eric reminded him.

"Oh yeah. I forgot. So tell me again anyway."

Eric plopped onto the overstuffed chair next to the couch where his buddy reclined. Putting his feet on the coffee table, Eric sat back and filled Jerome in on the latest football scoop. Coach had decided to put second-string Darnell Trott in for Jerome as wide receiver until the all-star athlete could return. Practices were grueling, but good, and the team had won its last three games. It looked like they were headed for the district title again this year—it was the same scoop Eric had recounted to Jerome an hour earlier, but it was new news to his confused friend.

Jerome had been forgetting a lot of things since he came home from the hospital. His thoughts were slow. His movements were slow. And his body didn't feel like his body anymore; it wouldn't listen to him. Though he'd never admit it, his mom was right: his legs felt wobbly beneath him. And he still felt dizzy. *I'm just out of shape and sore from my fall,* he rationalized. *And I'm just forgetful from sleeping so much. I'll be fine. I just need to get back to practice.*

Tommy returned with three slices of pizza, handing one each to his friends.

"Whoa." Tommy stared as Jerome lifted his pizza to his mouth. "Will you look at that!"

Eric and Jerome looked at the pizza Jerome lifted to his mouth. It quivered along with the trembling hand that held it. No matter how hard he tried, the former wide receiver, once called "Velcro hands" because of his ability to snatch, hold, and keep the ball steady, couldn't make his hand stay still.

"Good news." Dr. Wilkerson affirmed from across the desk in his office. Your most recent MRI is clean, Jerome, so that tremor shouldn't be permanent. But you need to be honest with me. Are you having any other trouble?"

Jerome looked as his mother, then at Jenny, who'd accompanied them to the doctor's office. "No," he lied. "I'm fine."

"He couldn't tie his shoes the other day," Jenny piped in.

"Shut up, squirt!" Jerome cast a threatening look at his little sister.

"Is that true, Jerome?" the neurologist persisted.

Jerome dropped his gaze. "I guess. Maybe. Whatever."

"Tell me what happened."

"Well, it was like . . ." He searched for words that seemed just out of reach. "Like, I could see myself tying my shoelaces in my mind . . . like, every step. . . . I could picture what I was supposed to do, but I couldn't make my fingers do what they were supposed to do. They could move okay, they just couldn't tie."

"Have you noticed anything else?"

Jerome shook his head.

Mrs. Johnson looked at her son, then at the doctor. "He seems unsteady, like he's off balance or something. And he's edgy all the time."

"Jerome?" the doctor persisted.

"I'm just tired, that's all. And sometimes my right leg feels weaker or like it's asleep. I just need to get back to practice and it'll strengthen up just fine."

"Look, son. As your doctor, I need you to be honest with me about what's happening to you. Only you can describe how you feel. No one else. Not your mom, not Jenny, not your dad. If I'm going to help you, you need to tell me about your symptoms, no matter how small or insignificant they seem. You've got to tell me."

His chair squeaked as Dr. Wilkerson leaned forward and set his folded hands on the blotter in front of him. He sighed. "Thankfully, **physical** and **occupational therapies** should be able to help the symptoms you describe. I fully expect you to regain your strength and coordination. Not to worry. Muscle weakness after a head injury isn't that uncommon, and it often passes."

The doctor paused, then completed his thought. "I'm actually more concerned about some of the other things your mother mentioned earlier."

Jerome looked at the doctor, then at his mom, and then at Jenny, then back at the neurologist. Dr. Wilkerson turned his attention to Mrs. Johnson.

"It sounds like Jerome is experiencing **post-concussive syndrome** or **PCS** for short. His lingering dizziness, persistent headaches, inability to concentrate, short-term memory problems, personality changes, difficulty reading, frequent rage—all of these are classic PCS symptoms. PCS usually clears up within the first few days or weeks of a head injury, and it's only been two weeks now. It could still clear up on its own." He turned and looked at Jerome.

Jerome couldn't track what they'd just been talking about. He felt angry and frustrated.

"I won't kid you, Jerome," the doctor continued. "For some people, PCS can last months, even years. For a few, for a very small percentage of TBI patients, the symptoms appear to be permanent. I don't think that's the case for you, though."

"When can I play football again?"

The physician sighed. "Well, I think you'd better plan on sitting out the rest of the season. You can't risk another head injury so soon, not with your lingering symptoms."

"What!" Jerome awkwardly shot out of his chair, sending it sprawling behind him. He steadied himself on the doctor's desk. "The whole season? You mean I can't play the whole season?" He leaned threateningly toward his doctor. "Nobody's gonna keep me from playing. Not you, not them," he ranted, gesturing toward his mother and sister, "not anybody."

"Calm down, Jerome," his mother interceded, resting her hand on her son's sleeve.

Flailing his arm to shake free of her touch, Jerome shrieked, "Don't tell me what to do! Don't *ever* tell me what to do."

Jerome's mother, Jenny, and the doctor looked at each other in stunned silence. The room was quiet except for the enraged teenager's panting. His outburst had taken every ounce of energy he had.

"I can't believe I blew up at the doctor like that," Jerome told Eric as they sat quietly in the empty football stadium. He leaned forward, planted his elbows on his knees, and sighed. Shaking his head, he continued. "I can't believe they won't let me play."

A cold November north wind tousled his hair, so he lifted his letter-jacket's collar to fend off the chill. It wasn't the good chill of post-exertion sweat like he'd experienced biking weeks earlier; this was the chill of cold realization. It penetrated his bones.

Eric sat on the cold, aluminum bleacher listening to his friend. Everyone else was right. Jerome *was* different since the accident. He wasn't the same old Germ he'd always been. Instead of being fun and confident, he'd become morose, angry, and insecure. Eric wasn't sure how to help. But at least he hung in there. Tommy, the third of their trio, had started avoiding Jerome altogether.

"Sounds like it's not a bad idea to me," Eric offered softly. "I mean . . ." He paused, looking for words, "Just take the season off so you can rest up and get better. You can still come to practices, hang out with the team—they still look up to you, you know. Just don't do anything that could make your head worse."

"Yeah, like play, right? So what's left? Should I become another Stevie stat boy?" There was no mistaking the sarcasm of his words.

"Stevie's not a bad kid. You might even like him."

Jerome sighed, started to stay something, stopped. Glancing away toward the empty football field, he stared silently for a moment. Then he began again. "The doc says I need to start rehab, and they want me to come after school. That means I'll miss practice most of the time. But I can stop by. Besides, I'm sure *Stevie's* got the bench under control." The bitterness in his voice was unmistakable.

LONG-TERM MOTOR PROBLEMS CAUSED BY TBI

In addition to headaches, dizziness, and memory problems, TBIs, even mild ones, can cause muscles to not function as they did before the injury. These injuries can interfere with the ability to stand, walk, sit, climb stairs, tie shoes, ride a bike, run, or do any number of tasks we normally take for granted. The most common muscle problems following TBI include:

- Poor motor coordination: the inability to control muscle movements or perform actions at the same speed and exactness as before the injury.
- Decreased muscle strength: weakness or difficulty with movement in a certain part of the body. Depending on the location of the brain's injury, specific parts of the body may be affected. *Hemiplegia* refers to paralysis in one side of the body (one hand, arm, and leg). *Hemiparesis* means weakness (instead of paralysis) in one side of the body. *Paraplegia* refers to paralysis of the lower half of the body (including both legs) resulting from spinal cord injury. *Diplegia* refers to weakness in corresponding parts of the body on both sides (both arms, both hands, both feet, or both legs). *Quadriplegia* describes paralysis of all four limbs. (The suffix *-plegia* refers to paralysis, and *-pareses* refers to weakness.)
- Increased or decreased muscle tone: when muscles are too tight or too relaxed. Changes in muscle tone can affect any or all quadrants of the body.

Paraplegic, Diplegic, Hemiplegic, or Quadriplegic?

Depending on the location of the brain injury, specific parts of the body may be affected. Often one side of the body is impacted, or just the upper or lower extremities may be involved. Doctors refer to these injuries this way:

Hemiplegia or Hemiparesis	Paraplegia
(hemi = one half, left or right)	(para = one half, from the waist down)

When Jerome's head hit the tree, the front part of his brain crashed into his skull, bruising his left frontal lobe. Since the left side of the brain controls the right side of the body, his left brain injury resulted in right-sided weakness and tremor. The bruising to the frontal lobe, in particular, also explains Jerome's short-term memory problems, his confusion, his inability to think clearly and logically, and his changes in personality and behavior. These functions are all handled by the brain's frontal lobes.

A person who is a paraplegic or quadraplegic will need a wheelchair to get around.

This boy's life was changed forever by a brain injury.

EFFECTS OF AN INJURED BRAIN

A brain injury can affect a person's:

thoughts
feelings
attitudes
actions
behavior
personality
physical abilities

SYMPTOMS OF POST-CONCUSSIVE SYNDROME (PCS)

amnesia
anger
concentration problems
decision-making problems
depression
disorganization
distractibility
dizziness
lack of emotional affect
emotional extremes (frequently changing emotions or
    intense emotions)
fatigue
flashbacks
headaches
memory loss, especially difficulty remembering new things
personality changes
sleep disturbances

TIMELINE FOR RECOVERY

Mild Brain Injury (Concussion)

Most people who sustain a mild TBI recover within days to a couple of weeks and have no permanent side effects. Some take longer to recover completely, but still do. A few never regain complete pre-injury function and may experience long-term or permanent consequences from their injuries.

Moderate Brain Injury

People who sustain a moderate TBI will almost always experience physical, cognitive, emotional, or behavioral side effects for several months after injury. In some cases, these impairments become permanent. Appropriate therapies

A person with a moderate brain injury will experience physical, cognitive, emotional, and behavioral side effects. Some of these will be permanent.

allow moderately brain-injured persons either to recover fully or to successfully learn to adapt and compensate for the injuries.

Severe Brain Injury

A severe brain injury usually results in prolonged coma (days, weeks, months, years). The individual who "wakes" from a coma can make significant progress in the first year after his injury. Progress can continue for several years after that, usually at a slower rate, but most people who have sustained severe TBIs end up with permanent physical, emotional, behavioral, or cognitive disabilities. The severity of these disabilities is impossible to predict, and outcomes vary with each person.

MY INJURY DOESN'T FEEL "MILD" TO ME!

Don't allow the term "mild" to confuse you. "Mild" closed-head injury or "mild" TBI does not mean "easily overcome" or "soon I'll be back to normal." "Mild" refers only to the extent of injury actually done to the brain during the initial trauma; it does not refer to the severity of symptoms you might experience later. It is possible to have a mild head or brain injury yet experience debilitating dizziness, inability to focus, muscle weakness, memory loss, or other symptoms.

COMMON REACTIONS FROM FRIENDS AND FAMILY

When a person sustains a brain injury, he isn't the only one affected; family and friends suffer, too. Reactions will vary and depend on the patient's injury, prognosis, and progress toward recovery. But most families and friends share similar responses.

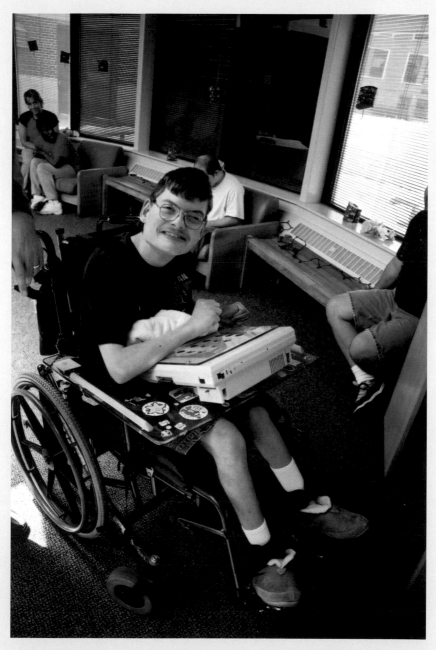

A brain injury can be an enormous challenge to overcome.

Shock/Denial

"How could this be?" or "I can't believe this is happening," or "I'm going to wake up and find out it was all a dream," are common initial reactions to hearing about a loved one's brain injury.

Helplessness/Fear of Losing Control

Circumstances seem out of control. Emotions feel unpredictable. Families often feel like there's nothing they can do to help their loved one's recovery or to prevent further injury.

When a child has sustained a brain injury, she may need to relearn basic skills, such as feeding herself.

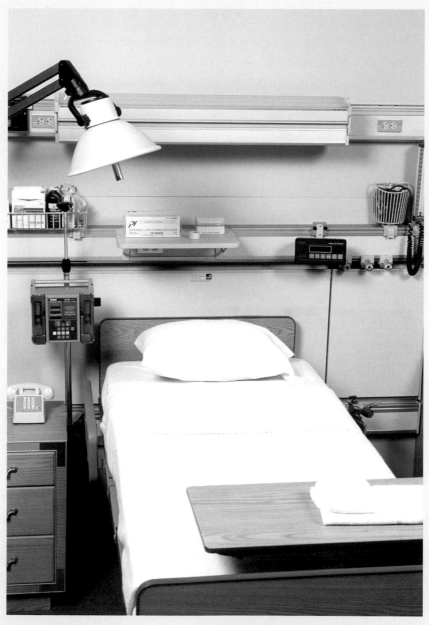

A hospital's unfamiliar equipment and surroundings may add to family members' anxiety.

Guilt/Blame

Parents, friends, and siblings will often think things like "It should have happened to me, not her" or "It's all my fault; if only I'd . . ." or "If only he hadn't . . ." Self-blame or blaming others are common responses to hearing of a loved one's injury.

Anxiety/Fear

Siblings, in particular, may ask "Will the same thing happen to me?" Parents may worry about recovery and long-term disability. Both fear the unknown.

COMMON WAYS OF FRUSTRATING THE PATIENT

Friends and loved ones often fall into patterns of behavior that can frustrate a person with a TBI. The most common and most frustrating include:

1. Minimization: "Oh, it's not that big a deal. Look how well you're doing. You'll be better in no time." This kind of comment, though well intended, negates the difficulty of the struggle for a patient with a TBI.
2. Denial: "You'll be your old self soon." Depending on the severity of injury, the person with a TBI may never be his "old self" again. TBI can permanently alter a person's mental abilities and personality. Pushing someone to be his "old self" puts him under impossible pressure to perform or to be something he can no longer be.
3. Catering: It's tempting to coddle people with brain injuries. But completing their sentences for them when speech is halting, or tying their shoes for them

when they are able but are taking too long, only impedes their progress. They may need to struggle with motor tasks and not do things perfectly or swiftly at first in order to regain their skills.

4. Avoidance: Just because a person with a TBI may look or act differently doesn't mean he doesn't need you or want you to be there. Yes, it may be uncomfortable at first, but the more time you spend together, the more comfortable you'll both become.

I'm here . . . to help people focus on their abilities, not their disabilities.
—Bill Johnson

4

ONE DAY AT A TIME

The air smelled stale and thick with sweat. It echoed with whirring treadmills and clanging workout machines. *Yup*, thought Jerome, *this is a gym all right*. It even looked like one, complete with exercise mats, Nautilus equipment, free weights, and room-size mirrors on one wall. The blue mats Jerome saw on the floor looked like the wrestling mats he'd seen at school, except without a white ring painted on them. Other mats rested on top of square tables set lower to ground. They reminded the teenager of large, square coffee tables covered with two-inch thick pads.

Mats on tables? Weird. This gym was definitely different.

In addition to the normal gear Jerome was used to seeing, he noticed other things: pulley weights on the wall; parallel bars; exercise balls; wheelchairs, crutches, and assorted braces; balance beams set three inches off the floor; four-step stairways with railings leading nowhere; and high, flat-top, wooden tables with assorted peg boards, towels, and hand weights resting on their surfaces. That seemed weird, too.

Jerome was entering a strange new world called rehab.

"Hi there! You must be Jerome," a friendly voice startled him out of his observations. He turned and saw a twenty-something guy with curly dark hair approaching with his hand extended. Jerome shook his hand, embarrassed by how weak his grasp was.

"I'm Matt, your physical therapist." Matt checked his clipboard and noted, "This is your first time here, right?"

"Yeah."

"Well, welcome to County Rehab! Looks like you've already noticed the gym. This is where we'll be doing most of our regimen. It's usually more crowded than this; you just happened to get here before the rush. Before we actually get started on any of this gym equipment, though, I need to do your intake interview, which basically gives me some background information. Let's hit one of the exam rooms, so we can talk a bit about what happened to you and what you can expect to get out of the rehab program. Just follow me."

"Whatever," Jerome mumbled as he fell in step behind the therapist.

The two young men walked through the gym and out into a narrow hall, which led to several rooms. They all seemed the same. Each room had neutral or pastel-colored walls that displayed assorted charts of various body parts. Toward the center of the room was a paper-covered exam table like Jerome had seen in his doctor's office, except that this table was shorter and had thicker pads on top. In one corner of the room, a rolling stool waited for the next doctor or therapist; in the other corner sat an empty folding chair.

"Hop up on the table, Jerome."

Jerome did as he was told.

"Your records tell me that you were in a biking accident just over two weeks ago." The physical therapist rolled the stool back and forth beneath him. "What can you tell me about what happened?"

"Nothing, really. I mean, I don't really remember. They told me I hit a dog and flew off my bike, and that I hit my head on a tree. But that's just what they told me."

"What about your stay in the hospital?"

"I don't remember much of that either, at least not until it was time for me to go home. I think they said I was in there two days."

"How about your symptoms since? What can you tell me about those?" Matt glanced at his notes, wrote something down, and then looked back at Jerome.

"Well, um, my right hand shakes, and, like, I can't always get it to do what I want it to do. Like, I know what I want it to do, but it won't do it. It's really frustrating."

"I'm sure it is. And that's just your right hand?"

"Mostly. But my legs feel wobbly or weak or something, mostly my right leg, though. It's hard to explain."

Matt listened attentively, occasionally jotting down notes. Now and then, he interjected a question, and Jerome answered as best he could. He told Matt about his headaches and dizziness, his memory problems, and his rage. Jerome could sense that Matt was an okay guy.

If anybody'll understand my need to get back to the team, Matt will, Jerome thought to himself. He decided to be honest.

"Look, all I want to do is play football again. Can you get me back on the team?"

Matt told Jerome to lie back on the table. "I can't answer that right now, Jerome. I need to do some preliminary evaluations so I can design your rehab. I have to assess what works and what doesn't work with your body." Matt's expression seemed to say he wasn't optimistic about Matt getting back to football this season. "Then we determine what you can and cannot do. The goal is to get you to do as many things as you did before, *maybe* even play football again, but we can't know that for sure right now. There are some things you might not be able to do like before, and for those things we'll teach you what we call **compensatory strategies** to work around your lingering limitations."

Jerome didn't understand a lot of what Matt said, but he heard, "play football again." That was all he needed to hear.

"So let's get started." Jerome was ready.

"Okay. Let's figure out what's working and what's not. This won't hurt. I promise. While you're lying down, lift your left foot and leg for me, okay?"

Jerome picked up his leg. Matt continued, "Hold it out straight, like a leg lift. Now, I'm going to push down on your leg, and I want you to try to keep me from pushing it back down. You push up against me. Got it? Okay, you ready? One . . . two . . . three . . . push!"

Jerome strained against his therapist's pressure. A few seconds passed.

"Great! You can relax. You've got a strong leg there! Good job. Now, let's try your right leg. Ready? One . . . two . . . three . . . push!"

Jerome resisted with everything he had, but his right leg lowered toward the table.

Matt and Jerome continued through several more exercises until the therapist felt he'd determined what he needed to know.

"The good news, Jerome, is that rehab can help you, if you work hard. The bad news is that you're not ready to play football. Not yet. You can use football as a goal to work toward, but there are no guarantees. Are you still willing to work at it?"

"Anything to get me back on the team."

Matt sighed. "Let's take this a day at a time, okay? We'll get you set up for PT and OT four or five days a week on alternating days. What do you say?"

"PT? OT?"

"Physical therapy and occupational therapy. We call them PT and OT for short."

"Oh, okay."

Matt and Jerome walked back down the hall and out to the gym. As they crossed the gym to the reception area where his mother was waiting and where they would set up his next appointments, someone called his name.

"Jerome? Hey Jerome, is that you?"

Jerome turned. The gym had filled up while he'd been in the exam room with Matt. An old lady with curly white hair sat in a wheelchair at one of the tall tables he'd seen earlier. She was scrunching and unscrunching a towel with her fingers while a fresh-faced, just-out-of-college-looking woman encouraged her. At the opposite end of the table stood an elderly man putting fat round pegs into a board with holes in it, while an aide stood ready to catch him if he grew unsteady on his feet. On one of the big square mat-covered tables, Jerome saw a kid with braces on both legs, who he guessed was about six years old, being rolled back and forth by his therapist. Another kid, maybe eleven or twelve, sat on an exercise ball where another therapist held his knees and thighs and rolled the ball left and right. The pre-teen had to keep correcting his posture to keep his balance on the ball.

Jerome couldn't make out where he heard his name. Then he heard it again.

"Yo, Jerome! Over here!"

Jerome looked, then groaned inside. There, on the far side of the gym, he saw someone nod in his direction from the leg press machine; it was none other than Steve Martinez.

THE ULTIMATE GOAL

After someone sustains a TBI, the primary goal of his rehabilitation is to improve his ability to function at home, at school, and in society to the maximum extent possible.

Rehabilitation

Rehabilitation, or "rehab," is the process used to help a patient regain functions he had before an injury or illness. The goal is to recover as much of the patient's previous ability as his injuries will allow. A person with a moderate or severe TBI, for example, may need to relearn how to walk or talk or dress himself. A person with a mild TBI may need help retraining his short-term memory skills. Rehabilitation is the word used to describe the treatment the patient receives to help him achieve these ends.

Who is involved in rehab?

The *patient* is always the most important player in rehab, but depending on the severity of the injury, the patient may have any or all of the following involved in his rehabilitation:

- the patient's physicians
- the patient's family and friends
- rehabilitation nurses
- psychologists (for thinking abilities, memory, attention span, etc.)
- physical therapists (for large muscle abilities like walking, sitting, etc.)
- occupational therapists (for small muscle abilities like writing, tying, cutting, etc.)
- speech or language pathologists (for speaking clearly, relearning how to talk, etc.)

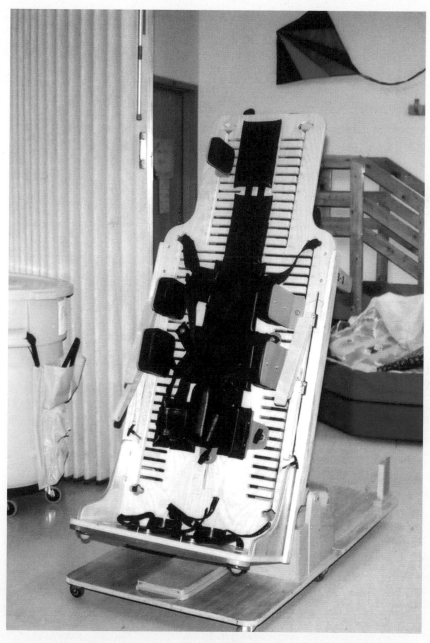

Many different kinds of equipment are used in rehab.

- dieticians or nutritionists (for appropriate menu planning and nutrition counseling)
- recreational therapists (for relaxation techniques and leisure skills)
- vocational rehabilitation counselors (to help with the transition to school or work)
- social workers (for connecting the patient with available resources and programs)

Where will I go for rehab?

If a TBI patient's injuries require her to be hospitalized, her rehab may begin in the hospital before she is released. After discharge, the location of the patient's rehab depends on her specific needs. Patients in need of rehab services can find them in a number of places:

Rehab centers are often bright, cheerful places filled with a variety of equipment.

- at home, when therapists make home visits
- at the hospital, as an out-patient
- at an acute rehab center, as an in-patient
- at a sub-acute rehab unit in a medical center, as an in-patient or out-patient
- at a rehab center or clinic, as an out-patient
- at a physician's office
- in school

Jerome's rehab took place at a sub-acute rehab center, which served short-term in-patients and out-patients like Jerome.

Assistive Devices You Might See in Rehab

- tilt-in-space wheelchairs with headrests, side supports, and seatbelts
- upright wheelchairs for patients with good head control but who need body support
- regular wheelchairs for patients who can sit upright and propel themselves
- electric wheelchairs for patients who can't propel themselves
- canes
- walkers
- crutches
- shoe inserts or lifts
- hand splints
- forearm splints
- slings
- ankle braces made of a single piece of lightweight plastic, called a molded **ankle-foot orthosis** (AFO or MAFO) or a two-piece AFO with a hinge at the ankle, called an Articulated Ankle-Foot Orthosis

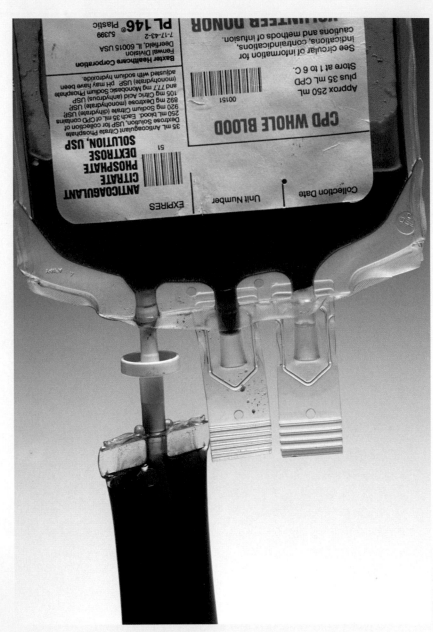

After a TBI, some patients may need blood transfusions or medication and nutrition through an IV.

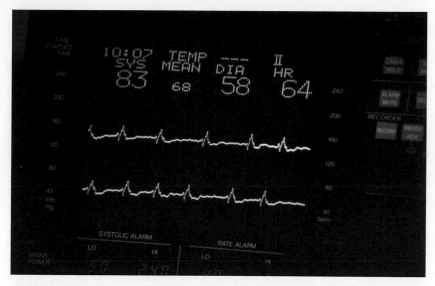

The vital signs of a person in a coma will often be monitored electronically.

OTHER COMPLICATIONS OF TBIs

Some patients with TBIs, especially with moderate or severe TBIs, will encounter complications that Jerome never faced. Some of these include:

- extended coma (unconsciousness for days, weeks, months, or even years)
- the need for a ventilator (being unable to breath without help from a machine)
- the inability to swallow or eat, hence the need for various feeding tubes:
    - nasogastric tube (NG tube): runs through the nose, down the throat, into the stomach; used when the patient has short-term eating difficulties.
    - gastrostomy tube (G tube): a tube put into the stomach through a hole in the abdominal wall or through the throat when there is a longer problem with eating.

- hydrocephalus (having too much spinal fluid in the brain, which creates too much pressure)
- the need for a shunt (a tube inserted into the brain cavity to drain excess fluid)
- seizures (disruptions in the brain's electrical activity that can cause abnormal movements, changes in levels of consciousness, and unusual sensations)
- permanent physical disabilities in one or more limbs

Patients with these complications require rehab, too, though their rehab may occur while they are still in a coma or recently out of a coma, but still in the hospital.

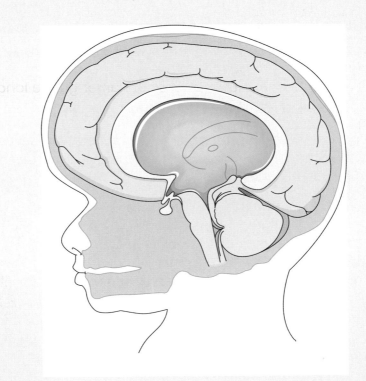

A person with hydrocephalus has too much spinal fluid in the brain.

TWELVE WAYS TO HELP SOMEONE THROUGH REHAB

1. Get involved. Go with the patient to rehab.
2. Learn about his condition.
3. Be positive.
4. Be realistic.
5. Be patient.
6. Praise/applaud successes, no matter how small.
7. Encourage small, manageable, short-term goals.
8. Keep records (photo, journal, scrapbook, etc.) to record progress.
9. Celebrate milestones with special outings or treats.
10. Hang in there when progress is slow or discouraging.
11. Encourage independence, but be there to help when truly necessary.
12. Remember to laugh; a sense of humor goes a long way toward healing.

Be of good cheer. Do not think of today's failures, but of the success that may come tomorrow.
—Helen Keller

5

THERAPY

"You guys know each other?" Jerome's physical therapist asked as he saw Steve Martinez nod to Jerome from across the room.

"Yeah, sort of," Jerome admitted reluctantly. He barely acknowledged the teen he knew as "Stevie stat boy."

Matt seemed to sense the discomfort in Jerome's manner and the embarrassment in his voice. "Steve's a good kid. Been through a lot. Has a great attitude. You might want to get to know him."

Matt turned to the receptionist to explain the kind of appointments Jerome needed for the next several weeks. Jerome's mother came in from the waiting room to take part in their discussion. Jerome turned his back to the gym and pretended to be involved in their dialogue.

I'll just ignore him, he thought as he avoided looking in Stevie's direction. *Why do people keep telling me I need to "get to know" Stevie? Somebody else did, too. Who was it? And they keep saying that he's a "good kid." Yeah, right. The kid's a dweeb; I don't want to "get to know" Stevie or anybody else for that matter; I just want this to be over and done with. I just want to play football again."*

Jerome felt a hand rest on his shoulder. He turned to see Stevie standing there.

"Hey, Jerome," Steve said, wiping the sweat off his forehead with a white exercise towel. "Sorry to see you here, man." His words were sincere.

Jerome looked at the sweating fifteen-year-old. *That's funny. Ste-*

vie seems taller and more muscular here. Next to the football team, he always looked so small.

Jerome didn't know what to say. He'd never had a real conversation with Stevie since the kid had moved into the district two years ago. And the last time he'd seen him was just before his accident when he'd tied Stevie's shoelaces to the bench. What could he say?

"Yeah, well, um . . . look, hey, I'm sorry about tripping you at practice a while back. I didn't mean anything by it. It was just a joke. Nothin' personal." It was the best he could come up with.

"Thanks, but don't sweat it," Steve offered, accepting the apology. "I'm used to people not knowing how to treat me. Besides, I've been through worse."

The two teenagers stood awkwardly facing each other, not really knowing what to say next. Then Steve jumped in. "So, anyway, welcome to the zoo!" He gestured broadly, acknowledging the whole gym.

"Zoo?" Jerome didn't get it.

"Yeah, the zoo. That's what I call it. A zoo has different species of animals, and the animals are all caged, sort of waiting to get out. Some are on loan; some are permanent exhibits. It's kind of like that here. You get all kinds of people in rehab: some are really bad off and come here for a long time; others just come for a few weeks and then move on. But nobody really wants to be here. We all want to get this behind us. We all want out."

"So why are you here?" Jerome asked

"Me? I'm a regular. A permanent exhibit, if you will. Well, sort of, I guess. I come back as I need to, like when I'm growing a lot or my body is changing and my muscles start getting all weird again."

"No, I mean, what made you need rehab?" Jerome persisted. He had never bothered to ask Stevie about his condition before or what made him walk the way he did. It never seemed important to know—or maybe he was too embarrassed to ask. Now, he really wanted to know.

"Oh that. I nearly drowned three years ago. Well, that's not entirely true. I did drown. They tell me I was under the water for several minutes and that I was dead when they pulled me out. They did **CPR** and got my heart going again, but I was in a coma for six days, on a **ventilator** and everything. They still don't know what made me come out of it. My mom says it was a miracle. I don't know. I can't remember."

Jerome was surprised as he listened to Stevie describe his "death" so matter-of-factly. It was almost like they were talking about the weather or the next football game.

"But, anyway, when I woke up, I couldn't walk or talk or do any of the stuff I did before. There I was—a twelve-year-old who couldn't feed himself or pee on his own. They thought I'd be a vegetable. But I relearned it all. Took a long time, though." Steve fingered his towel and glanced at the floor. They both stood silently for a minute. Then Steve looked up and continued.

"I got most everything back, I think, except my 'land legs.' They tell me that the muscle weakness I have in my legs is permanent. That's why I wear these."

Steve lifted his sweatpants to reveal something Jerome had never noticed before. Molded plastic braces covered the sides and backs of Steve's lower legs and ankles. Wide Velcro straps across his shins held the braces in place. It looked like the braces extended into his shoes. Jerome noted a metal hinge at each ankle.

"They're called articulated ankle foot orthothoses or AFOs. They keep my feet from dropping. Without them, my toes drop, and then I trip. My muscle weakness keeps me from being able to pull my toes up on my own."

"Hey, sorry, man. I didn't know," was all Jerome could mumble.

"Like I said, don't sweat it. You couldn't have known. All you saw was a geeky kid who tripped a lot. I understand. Believe me, I do. I used to be a lot like you, in fact."

That last comment caught Jerome's attention. "Whaddya mean?"

"Before the accident, I could've *been* you. That was before we moved here. I was popular and athletic. I was pretty good at peewee soccer and midget football. They tell me I was the best wide receiver

the midget league ever had." Steve looked Jerome in the eye. Jerome
held his gaze for a second but then looked away.

"I even picked on the geeks, just like you." Steve looked at
Jerome. There was no malice in his eyes, only honesty. Jerome didn't
know what to say.

"But that was the old Steve, and that Steve drowned three
years ago. He'll never be back. It's taken a long time for me to accept that, but I'm okay with it now. What you see now is the new,
improved model." Steve spread his arms wide, then, folding one
arm in front of him and swooping his towel in front of him, he
bowed dramatically.

Improved? What does he mean? Jerome decided his brain must
still be too shook up to understand what Steve was saying.

"Who's this?" Jerome's mother interrupted. She, Matt, and the
receptionist had finished plotting Jerome's therapy schedule. "Friend
from school?"

"Um, well, yeah. . . . Stevie's the guy who keeps the books for
the football team," Jerome mumbled.

"Hi, Mrs. Johnson. My friends call me *Steve*." He introduced
himself, casting a glance at Jerome and emphasizing that his name
was Steve, not Stevie. "Nice to meet you."

"And you, too, Steve," Jerome's mother replied, shaking Steve's
hand. Then turning to her son, she reminded him, "We need to get
going. Jenny's waiting for us to pick her up at her friend's house."

"Oh yeah, uh, I forgot." *It seems like I always forget.*

"Well, I guess I'll see you around," Steve offered. "Gotta get
back to my weights." He turned and hobbled back to the Nautilus machines on the other side of the gym. Jerome stared after
him.

"Oh, and Jerome," Steve called back over his shoulder. "Rehab
may be tougher than you think. If you ever want to talk or work out
together or anything, you know where I am."

Yeah, right. Jerome thought to himself, but he nodded and tried
to smile.

The next several days became a blur of school, homework, and re-hab for Jerome. Returning to school was more difficult than he imagined it would be. He just couldn't think clearly or remember the things the teachers were teaching. He forgot new assignments and had trouble organizing his work. Note taking, with the weakness in his right hand and his poor coordination, was nearly impossible. He relied on Eric to copy class notes for him, but Jerome was still falling way behind. And on top of his schoolwork, he had to go to rehab.

The "zoo" held Jerome captive two hours a day, four and five days a week after school. Sometimes he worked with Matt, and sometimes he worked with Gillian, his new occupational therapist. Jerome didn't realize that something as simple as buttoning, unbuttoning, and buttoning again could be so exhausting. Or tying and untying. Or holding a pen. Nothing was as simple as it used to be. His coordination and strength just weren't the same. And he was still tired. Really, really tired.

Today's therapy wasn't going well. Jerome swore as he threw the lacing board he'd been working on down on the table. He'd been doing OT for thirty minutes already and wasn't getting anywhere.

"I know you're frustrated, Jerome," Gillian sympathized, "but you don't need to swear. Just take a deep breath, blow it out slowly, and try again." She handed the lacing board back to him.

Gillian was working with Jerome on strengthening his hands. She had him squeezing rubber balls, putting pegs into a pegboard, scrunching towels with his hands, and working with finger weights. This time she had him working on the lace board. It was a simple device, really, just a square, lightweight plastic board designed to look like the top of a shoe. Permanently attached to the board were two laces, just like you'd have at the top of a sneaker. Jerome's assignment was to tie the laces on the fake shoe. He had yet to succeed and had grown increasingly more frustrated with each failed attempt.

"I'm not doing this anymore. I can't do it!"

Jerome panted with effort and frustration as thoughts raced through his brain. *I can walk. I can even run pretty well, now. I'm not so dizzy anymore. Why can't I tie my shoes? When am I going to be like I used to be? Will I ever be normal? Why can't I just get better?*

His recovery had been like this. Some things seemed fine, nearly back to normal, causing Jerome to think he'd be "fixed" in no time at all. Then other things, like muscle coordination in his hands, didn't seem to improve. When he had trouble, he fell into cycles of anger, helplessness, frustration, and despair.

This latest round of frustration drove Jerome to make a decision, one he'd been toying with since he started rehab. *I'm going back to practice,* he thought with determination. *If anything will make me better, getting back in shape with the team will.*

Steve watched from the other side of the rehab gym. He couldn't read Jerome's thoughts, but he knew his frustration. He'd been there. He knew what it was like. Jerome was in for a difficult time, Steve was sure. Just tying and retying the laces would sap Jerome's strength and concentration, as it had Steve's years ago. He also knew that Jerome expected too much too soon. If he didn't settle down, he'd only make it harder for himself. Steve knew all this. He'd already been through it.

Steve thought about approaching Jerome again. Jerome needed someone who understood what he was going through. Most old friends, Steve knew from experience, found it too hard to hang in there when the person they saw today wasn't same person they had known before. Most would give up and move on. Jerome would need a friend. But Steve had tried once already, and Jerome, though civil, had kept his distance. Steve would wait until Jerome was ready.

That day would come sooner than either boy expected.

HOW LONG DOES REHAB TAKE?

Though there is no set timetable for rehab, the effects of a brain injury usually show the greatest and most rapid improvement within the first six to nine months after injury. After the first year, a patient can still show progress, but it will be slow, and the gains will be less noticeable.

WAYS THE BRAIN CAN BE INJURED

A traumatic injury to the brain, like Jerome sustained, is not the only cause of brain injury. Brain injuries fall into two main categories: *congenital injuries* (those present at birth) and *acquired injuries* (injuries not present at birth that result from an external force, illness, or event; TBIs fall into this category). Each category represents several different types of brain injury. They could be diagrammed this way:

ALL BRAIN INJURIES

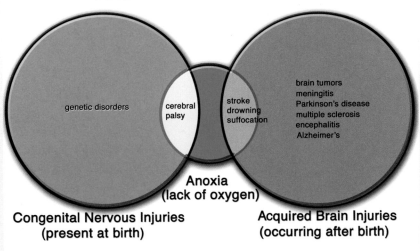

Near Drowning and Brain Injury

When a person nearly drowns, the brain is not injured the way it is in an accident or a blow to the head. In the case of an accident, the individual sustains a TBI; in a near drowning, the brain is injured from a prolonged lack of oxygen called **anoxia**. The impact of anoxia on the brain can be every bit as destructive as a TBI. Prolonged anoxia can be fatal.

OCCUPATIONAL THERAPY VS. PHYSICAL THERAPY

Area of Focus Type of Skill	Occupational Therapy **fine motor skills**	Physical Therapy **gross motor skills**
muscles	smaller muscle coordination, primarily upper body and limbs (especially hands and fingers)	large muscle groups, primarily lower limbs and trunk, overall fitness
activities	**activities of daily living (ADLs)**: feeding, grooming, dressing, bathing, writing, opening jars or bottles, cooking, using a keyboard or telephone, etc.	ability to move: rolling, sitting, standing, and becoming independent with walking or using adaptive equipment (crutches, canes, wheelchairs, etc.)
adaptive equipment	hand splints; wrist splints; adapted seats or chairs; special switches for computers or power wheelchairs; adapted devices for everyday use (electric scissors, fat grip pens, etc.); adapted self-care items	AFOs and other leg or ankle splints; leg braces; body braces; crutches or canes; electric or manual wheelchairs; walkers; adapted seating devices

ACTIVITIES YOU MIGHT SEE IN OCCUPATIONAL THERAPY

Depending on the patient's age and severity of injury, you might see a patient in OT doing any or all of the following:

- squeezing rubber balls or hand grips
- putting pegs into pegboards or putting puzzles together
- coloring or writing
- clenching and unclenching their hands
- pushing keys on a keyboard with their fingers
- tying or lacing
- manipulating zippers
- brushing or combing an animal or fake fur
- opening and closing pockets (using Velcro or buttons)
- putting lids on jars; opening and closing jars
- stacking blocks

Squeezing a rubber ball may be part of occupational therapy.

- scrunching and unscrunching a towel
- putting clothespins on a string
- using manual or electric scissors
- folding paper
- pouring, spooning, or ladling rice, pudding, or water from cup to cup
- using straws (for sipping, blowing, etc.)

ACTIVITIES YOU MIGHT SEE
IN PHYSICAL THERAPY

Depending on the patient's age and severity of injury, you might see a patient in PT doing any or all of the following:

- stretching or having the therapist stretch their muscles for them
- rolling from side-to-side on an exercising mat
- standing and sitting
- using an exercise ball
- "walking" on their hands, with legs resting on an exercise ball
- lifting free weights or using pulley weights
- stepping up and down stairs
- walking across a balance beam or tape mark on the floor
- throwing and catching a ball
- pulling, rowing, or playing tug-o-war
- practicing wheelchair maneuvers
- practicing using a walker or cane
- walking short distances with assistance or using parallel bars
- using Nautilus equipment
- walking on a treadmill
- riding an exercise bike
- swimming or using a hot tub

TEN QUALITIES OF A GOOD REHAB PROGRAM

A good rehab program includes:

1. A ***multidisciplinary team*** approach that includes the patient and parents as equal participants with professionals. This team may be made up of the patient's physician(s), occupational and physical therapists, speech pathologist, social worker, educational psychologist, and other professionals vested in the patient's treatment plan. The patient and parents are key members of this team who should be treated with courtesy and respect and encouraged to provide input.
2. Patient, parental, and family involvement in all aspects of the rehab program.
3. A commitment by all team members to work toward the patient's fullest potential.
4. Agreement among all team members about the course of the rehab plan.
5. A willingness to adapt, compromise, or change plans as needed.
6. Clear, consistent, and timely communication between team members.
7. A willingness to advocate for the patient in outside venues (school, work, etc.).
8. A plan for the patient to regain as much function as possible or to learn new compensation strategies that will enable him to gain the most independence.
9. An overall tone of realistic optimism.
10. A valuing of the patient for who they are today, not who they once were.

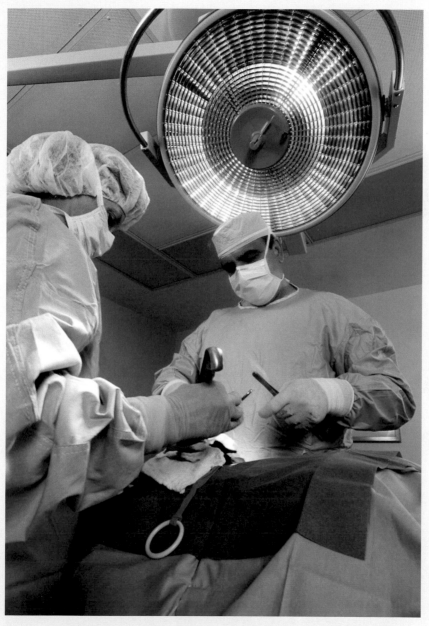

After the surgeon does his job, many other professionals will be involved in a patient's journey toward recovery.

RETURNING TO SCHOOL

Because TBIs can affect thinking, motor skills, memory, and other functions necessary for learning, a person with ongoing symptoms after a TBI may have difficulty returning to school. Before reentry to former classes, a TBI patient should have a complete educational assessment. This assessment should evaluate his fine motor skills, gross motor skills, long-term recall, short-term memory, reading ability, comprehension skills, ability to follow directions, speech and language skills, vision, hearing, and any other areas related to the student's injuries or school performance.

Many children with brain injuries will require special intervention designed to meet their needs.

Depending on the results of these assessments, a student with a TBI may need *special education* services, including an *individualized education plan (IEP)*. Special laws require school districts to provide free, appropriate education for students with disabilities that is tailored to meet the students' needs. Students with TBIs often discover they have new learning disabilities as a result of their injuries, and schools must do what is necessary to accommodate those needs.

Sometimes, the truth can be a bitter pill to swallow. But as Jesus of Nazareth said, the truth sets us free.
—Emily Binney

6

RUNNING INTO REALITY

"Hey, Johnson! Welcome back!" Coach called when he spotted Jerome crossing the practice field toward the huddle where team members had each dropped to one knee while awaiting the coach's instructions. Every helmeted head turned to look at their former wide receiver.

"So, you joining us, finally? It's only two weeks 'til districts."

Toward the edge of the huddle, Eric watched his best friend stride toward the team. And he heard the whispers.

"Johnson's back?"

"I thought he was out for the rest of the season."

"Somebody said he can't catch anymore. Is it true?"

Eric noticed a slight unevenness in Jerome's gait. No one else noticed, but Eric could see. The weakness in his friend's right leg was still there. Improving, maybe, but definitely there. That meant his right hand was still weak, too.

Eric got up and ran to greet his teammate and friend.

"What are you doin' here, man?" Eric whispered as they crossed the rest of the field.

"Comin' to practice. Whaddya think?"

"Look, Germ, I want you here more than anybody, you know that. But you're not ready. You know you're not. The docs said so." Eric's hushed voice was strained with urgency. "You could get hurt."

"Look, I'm fine. Just get off it. I know what I'm doing." Jerome thrust his duffle bag into his friend's arms and trotted up to the huddle. The other players stood up and greeted their returning star. Some shook his hand, some patted his helmet and shoulder pads, others high-fived him or smacked his butt the way football players do. Johnson was back.

Steve Martinez sat quietly on the bench, stat book in hand, watching the camaraderie. He caught Eric's eye, and they exchanged worried glances. Both knew that what would come next would be painful to watch, and even more painful for Jerome to go through. This had disaster written all over it.

"Okay. Party's over." Coach turned to Jerome. "You sure you're ready to play, Johnson?"

"You bet, Coach. Doctors and rehab say I'm good to go."

Eric and Steve winced. They knew Jerome was lying, but they also knew it would do no good to say anything. Jerome would have to learn the hard way.

"Okay then. You and Trott toss the ball a bit to get warmed up. Then we'll put you in a scrimmage."

"Yes sir, Coach." Jerome nodded, grabbing a football.

"Yo, Johnson! I already got a ball," Darnell called. Darnell Trott had been Jerome's replacement as wide receiver since Jerome got hurt. Unlike most of the team, the up-and-coming wide receiver wasn't happy about Jerome's return.

Jerome set his football down and walked over to the sideline where his replacement stood waiting, tossing the pigskin from one hand to the other.

"Think quick!" Darnell flipped the ball to Jerome. Jerome stood no chance of reacting fast enough, and the ball bounced off his face-mask. Eric and Steve witnessed their friend's embarrassment; no one else had seen the incident. Jerome bent over to pick up the football.

"Yeah, right. You're back." Darnell sneered. He leaned over Jerome as Jerome retrieved the ball and whispered, "All I can say is, you better be ready to play, and play hard. I'm not givin' up my spot so easy."

He turned and strode away, and the two wide receivers lined up on opposing forty-yard lines. Jerome fingered the ball in his hands for a second, then tossed a wobbling lob to his competition.

"Good thing you're not quarterbacking," Darnell scoffed. "Let's see if you catch any better than you throw." He bulleted the ball right at Jerome's numbers.

The football hit his chest. Jerome fumbled it a bit, but hung on.

"I'm just warming up. I can out catch you any day. Always could. That's why I started and you were second string." Jerome yelled back at Darnell as he threw another wobbling lob. It barely reached Darnell.

"Okay, hot shot. Catch this, then!" Darnell threw the ball hard. The perfect spiral flew straight for Jerome's head. Jerome threw his hands up to grab the pass, but he was too slow, his fingers too weak. The ball passed through his grasp and nailed him in the head. The former "Velcro hands" fell backward and landed in a heap on his back.

"What were you thinking?" Jerome's father raged.

Jerome's head obviously was hurting again. Eric sat next to him, feeling his friend's shame.

"You could've gotten yourself killed, or put yourself in a coma!" Mrs. Johnson said. "You know the doctors said you weren't ready to return. Even your therapists said so."

"But, Mom, Dad, I thought I could play. I really did. And I only got hit in the face. I didn't get knocked out or anything. Did I, Eric?"

Eric shook his head. No, Jerome hadn't been knocked out. Not this time. But he could've been.

"Don't you get it? You're out for this season, maybe for good. Get football out of you head; it's not happening. That's final." His father looked at Jerome, shook his head, then walked out of the family room. His mom looked at Jerome for a moment longer, then followed her husband.

Jerome and Eric sat in silence until they heard a soft knock at the sliding glass door. Steve Martinez was looking in at them; he slid the door open a crack. "I thought you might be able to use another friend right about now."

After Jerome missed Darnell's pass at practice, the team's response to their former all-star changed. He wasn't a returning hero anymore; he was just somebody who made them feel uncomfortable. No one wanted to look at him or talk to him. Even his lifelong friend Tommy seemed weird with him. They all left him alone.

Coach pulled Jerome aside and told him to take the rest of the practice, and the rest of the season, off. Jerome realized he no longer had a place on the team. He wasn't wanted there. Only Eric seemed to want him around anymore. And now Steve. Maybe Matt and Eric had been right. Maybe Steve wasn't such a bad kid after all. Maybe it wouldn't hurt to get to know him.

"I suppose I could," Jerome finally admitted. "Come on in."

SUSCEPTIBILITY TO RE-INJURY

Once an individual sustains a concussion or TBI, he runs a greater risk of sustaining a second concussion or TBI, even with less force or trauma to the head than in the original injury. Football players who sustain brain injuries, for example, are six times more likely to sustain new brain injuries than football players who have never sustained a concussion or TBI. Multiple brain injuries can result in permanent brain damage or even death.

Most doctors recommend that a child or teen who has sustained a moderate TBI not take part in contact sports for a least one year following the injury.

HOW TO TREAT A FRIEND WITH TBI

1. Accept his differences. Ask a physician about the medical reasons behind your friend's physical, emotional, and behavioral changes. Read all you can about his injury. Realize that someone with a TBI goes through many stages of recovery. The more you know, the easier it will be for you to accept the changes in your friend.
2. Grieve your loss. The person you once knew may never return. Some changes in a person with a TBI can be permanent.
3. Talk about the changes. Ask your friend how he feels. Be honest about how you feel, about your sadness. It's okay to say "I miss the old you."
4. Help your friend set realistic goals, and be there to help him achieve them.
5. Get to know the new person your friend has become. Avoid making comparisons with who he used to be. Appreciate the positive traits you see in this new person, and affirm the abilities he still possesses.

After a brain injury, both the individual and her family will need to adjust to her new abilities and limitations.

6. Consider getting counseling or joining a support group for loved ones of TBI patients.

THREE STAGES OF RECOVERY

Patients with TBIs go through similar stages in their recovery process:

Phase One: Becoming aware of the extent of the injury, and not just the original injury, but its long-term consequences as well. Denial, anger, depression, grief may all be part of this phase.

Phase Two: Accepting that some consequences may be permanent. This includes coming to grips with the "death" of the old self and the acceptance of the new. This is often the most difficult and longest lasting phase.

Phase Three: Regaining independence. After accepting the long-term changes a TBI can bring, the patient can learn or develop new strategies that enable him to become independent, grow in self-confidence, and work toward his potential.

QUOTE FROM A FATHER WHO'S BEEN THERE

"People who suffer serious traumatic brain injury rarely regain every level of functioning. But in virtually all cases, with proper treatment, they can improve with time."
—Nathan Aaseng, whose thirteen-year-old son Jay cracked his head on ice during a sledding accident and suffered a severe TBI

The will to conquer is the first condition of victory.
—Marshal Ferdinand Foch

7

HARD WORK AND DETERMINATION

"I don't know what I was thinking," Jerome admitted to Eric and Steve while the threesome sat in his family room drinking sodas and devouring pizza. Since the bike accident, Jerome constantly craved pizza and ordered it whenever his friends were around.

Eric and Steve had been there since Jerome's father brought him home from his failed practice attempt earlier that afternoon. It was another pizza night. Good thing, too. Jerome's head still hurt from being nailed with the football. Pizza was the only thing that tasted good to him right now.

"I guess I just thought if I could practice again, I'd get stronger," he mumbled between bites.

"It was a stupid thing to do, Germ. You really could've gotten hurt again," Eric said.

"Well, it looks like I won't be playing football any time soon anyway. Coach doesn't want to see me again 'til next year." He couldn't hide his disappointment.

"Jerome," Steve cut in hesitantly. As the newcomer, Steve was uncertain how much he could say. He decided he'd better spill what he was thinking—for Jerome's sake. Somebody had to say it. He mustered his courage, cleared his throat, and dove in.

"Look, you may have to accept the fact that you might not *ever* play football like you did before." Steve tried to be gentle. "Yeah, you can still get stronger, I know that's what Matt said, and your tremor is better—see, rehab really does work!" He grinned at his fellow zoo member, but then grew serious again. "Even after you finish rehab, you might not have the speed and reaction times you had before you got hurt. That's just the way it is with brain injuries. Believe me, I know."

Jerome looked at Steve. He'd never noticed how strong his features were. He'd never noticed the kindness in his eyes. He was beginning to see Steve, the *real* Steve, for the very first time.

But Steve wasn't finished.

"That doesn't mean you can't do anything well again. It doesn't mean that you don't have something to offer. I mean, football? Who cares? Five years from now nobody's gonna remember who was on the high school football team. You have a lot more to offer than how well you used to catch the ball."

Steve, the once-drowned, once-"dead," former-wide-receiver Steve, was probably the only one who could have said those words to Jerome. Jerome listened. He listened because he knew that Steve knew what it was like to lose what was important to you. Steve knew what it was like to give up your dreams. He knew what it was like to not know who you were anymore. And he knew what it was like to fear who you would become.

Jerome looked at the pizza in his now-still hand and said nothing. Eric decided to say something too. "Look, Germ. It took my mom nearly dying for me to realize that there's more to life than football and more to people than what they can do or what we can see. I tried to explain it to you before, but you just didn't get it."

Jerome recalled his confusion over Eric's changes since his mother got cancer. Now he was beginning to understand.

"So, you're different than you used to be, so what?" Eric continued. "My mom changed after her cancer. *I* changed after her cancer. *You* changed after your accident. We're all changing, but that doesn't mean we can't have new dreams. And it doesn't mean we're not still friends."

Eric paused, as if struggling for words, and then continued. "Sure, I miss some of the things that were the 'old you.' I'd be lying if I didn't admit that. But I like some of the 'new you' even better."

"Like what?" Jerome eyed his old friend suspiciously.

"Well, you're a lot less cocky than you used to be, for one. And you order a lot more pizza. That's another." Eric reached for another slice of pepperoni and cheese.

Jerome laughed, despite his anger and fear.

"You've just gotta give yourself, the *new* self, a chance," Steve said.

Jerome took a deep breath. Part of him wanted to hold on to his anger; that part wanted to swear and hit and break something. But almost to his surprise, he heard another part of him say, "Okay, football's out. So anybody want to go to the movies with the *new* me? At least there, I don't have to catch anything, and I can still down a bucket of popcorn with the best of them! We can even get more pizza."

All three sensed that a new triad, a new circle of friendship, had been formed in that room: one born of loss, but which they knew held great promise.

Over the next several weeks, Jerome settled into a routine—school during the day, rehab in the afternoon, homework and rest at night. He still battled fatigue, muscle weakness, headaches, occasional dizziness, and memory problems, but regular OT and PT seemed to improve his symptoms. Many PCS symptoms remained, but Jerome accepted them as part of the process, and he learned strategies to help him cope.

The football fiasco made Jerome realize that everything wasn't the same as it had been before his accident, nor would it be. *He* wasn't the same. Accepting his limitations allowed him to learn new ways of dealing with the changes. Having friends like Eric and Steve helped. They were always full of helpful ideas.

"Yo, try using sticky notes," Steve suggested when Jerome couldn't remember what time his rehab appointments were. "Write your appointment days and times on a note and put it on your mirror. You'll remember then."

"Try writing your combo on the inside sole of your shoe," Eric suggested when Jerome kept asking his friend what his locker combination was. After years of raiding each other's lockers, Eric knew Jerome's combination by heart.

His two friends even chipped in and bought Jerome a hand-held computer, sometimes called a **PDA**. It fit nicely in the side pocket of his cargo pants, so Jerome could take it anywhere with him, allowing him to write down his assignments and rehab dates when they were given. The PDA even had built-in alarms, which would sound to remind him of what to do and when to do it.

Support and tips from his therapists, family, and friends allowed Jerome to function, and function well, despite his challenges. Life after his TBI was possible, he began to realize. With the help of his friends, doctors, and rehab therapists, he figured out how to make this new life work. It was like getting on a bike again, he learned: some things were the same, some were different. But you pedaled forward anyway, and with each down stroke you gained momentum. Sure, there were steep inclines and rocky sections that made you want to quit, and you got really tired sometimes, but with hard work and determination Jerome was certain he could ride this trail to its end.

He didn't realize that he still had one steep hill to climb.

POST-TBI CRAVINGS

It isn't uncommon for an individual who has sustained a TBI to crave odd things. For Jerome it was pizza. Author Kara L. Swanson, whose book *I'll Carry the Fork!* recounts her recovery from a mild TBI caused by an auto accident, describes her unusual cravings this way:

> I craved things. Weird things. Things I never really ate before the accident. White chocolate and lobster and pancakes and oatmeal. Corned beef hash and fried egg sandwiches. I ate plain, canned, boiled potatoes for three weeks straight at one stretch.

TIPS FOR IMPROVING OR WORKING WITH MEMORY CHALLENGES

- Play memory card games with friends or on the computer ("Concentration," "Memory," or "Match Game," for example).
- Carry a notepad with you at all times and *write things down*. Keep your notepad in the same place for easy reference (the same pocket, or the same section of a purse, etc.).
- Use a mini tape recorder to record important meetings with doctors or other professionals. This will help you remember their key instructions.
- Use self-adhesive sticky notes for reminders. Post them on your bathroom mirror, refrigerator door, or anywhere you're likely to see them.
- Create checklists. To remember what to take to school, for example, create a list of what you need for each day of the week, and post it by the front door. Check the list before you leave each day.

- Wear a watch that tells the date, day of the week, and time.
- Do one thing at a time. Finish one task before moving on to the next.

A HELPFUL ELECTRONIC DEVICE

Personal digital assistants (PDAs) can help a TBI survivor with memory or organizational challenges. These hand-held computers do four basic tasks: manage contact information (names and addresses); keep track of appointments and important dates (calendars); maintain "to-do" lists (tasks); and provide the ability to take notes (notepads). The more expensive PDA models can also play music from MP3 files, make brief voice recordings, host

At a rehab center, a patient will learn new strategies for coping with life.

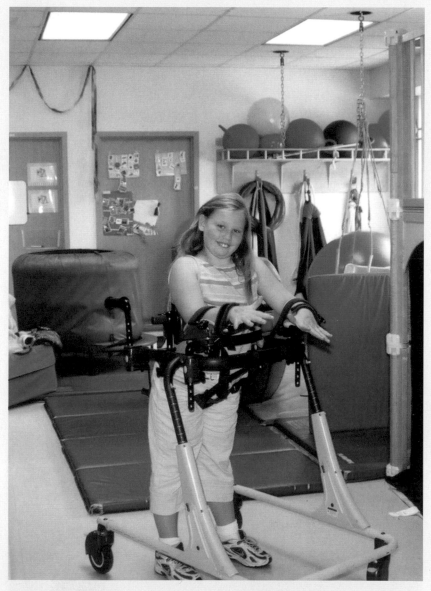

Learning to walk again may at first seem like the biggest challenge after a brain injury. But learning to keep track of time and remember important chores may prove to be even more difficult obstacles to overcome.

games, be used as a wireless telephone, function as a camera, and make wireless connections for using the Internet. The average price for a good, basic model runs between $100 and $300.

STRATEGIES FOR COPING WITH DIZZINESS

Ongoing bouts of dizziness can be a consequence of TBIs. Though you should always consult with your doctor about lingering symptoms, you can do some things at home to

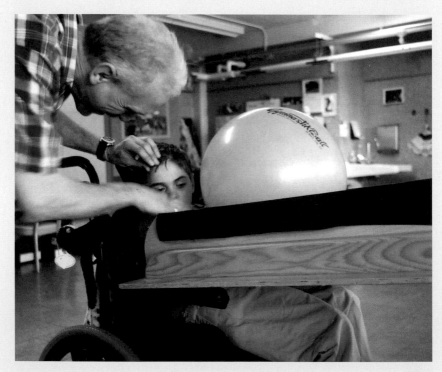

Pushing a large ball up a slight slope helps rebuild arm muscles.

ease the frequency and severity of dizzy spells. Most doctors suggest the following:

- When you start to feel dizzy, immediately stop moving and sit or lie down.
- Change positions slowly (e.g., lying to sitting, or sitting to standing, turning, etc.).
- Keep track of when you feel the most dizzy. Is it when you're tired, hungry, hot? Then take steps to avoid the conditions that seem most linked to your dizziness.
- Limit salt intake. Salt can make you retain fluids, which can increase your susceptibility to dizziness.
- Drink plenty of water. Dehydration can cause dizziness.
- Avoid alcohol or other recreational drugs. These will only worsen your symptoms.

When the old tracks are lost, new country is revealed. . . .
—Rabindranath Tagore

8

HIDDEN GIFTS

The air felt cool against Jerome's skin as he breezed along the tree-lined trail. A bright sun streamed through its leafy filter. Squirrels and chipmunks scattered at the sound of mountain bike tires kicking up cinders and ash. It felt so good to be back on a bike again. . . .

Jerome's legs felt strong, his balance good. The weakness in his right side was gone. Just to be sure, he squeezed his right brake. Yep, that hand was fine. He glanced over his shoulder at his two friends. Like always, they struggled to keep up with him. Jerome always was the fastest rider. Always would be. Yes sir, it was a fine day. A fine day indeed.

Up ahead the bushes stirred. No. It couldn't be. Jerome's heart pounded in his chest. Sweat pooled on his brow. He started panting. It felt like he couldn't breathe. There it was: the same black lab, the same leash, the same looming sycamore tree.

Oh no, not now. Not again. Not when I'm doing so well.

Like a third-person observer to the scene, he watched himself collide with the dog, catapult off his bike over the handlebars, and then . . . nothing, just the blinding white flash of impact.

Jerome awoke in a cold sweat. The nightmare was the third one this week.

"I hate these dreams," Jerome confided to Matt during their next physical therapy session. He paused, then started again. "But I suppose I like them, too."

Matt looked up at him. "How come?"

"Well . . ." Jerome searched for the right words. "Just for a minute . . . you know . . . for the few seconds in my dream right before I hit the tree, I feel like my old self again. My hand and leg are strong. My balance is good. I feel so free! But it doesn't last. It just becomes a nightmare all over again." He sighed.

"Nightmares and flashbacks are a normal part of recovery, Jerome." Matt explained. "Many people with TBIs experience them."

"But why am I having them now? I didn't for the first few weeks."

"I think it has to do with your memory coming back. It's been, what, six weeks now? You're remembering the actual event and not just what other people have told you about it. That's a good thing," the therapist reassured him. "You're healing."

"But I still have headaches."

"And you will. For a while, I bet. It's all part of it."

"So when will the nightmares end?"

"That I can't say," Matt admitted. "But I've heard that revisiting the place of the accident helps sometimes. It's like being there creates a new memory somehow. Have you been back to the trail since you got hurt?"

"No."

"You should think about it."

"What, now? It's December."

"Hasn't snowed yet. And it's still pretty mild. I'd be willing to drive you up to the trail head on Saturday if you'd like to give it a go."

Matt showed up as promised. He pulled into the Johnsons' driveway and found not only Jerome waiting there for him but Eric and Steve as well. The three teens piled into Matt's SUV, joking and talking as Matt pulled out of the driveway. As they neared the railroad trail's park entrance, though, they grew quiet. No one was sure what to expect.

Matt pulled into the parking lot by the ranger station, the same ranger station that Jerome's old friend Tommy had gone to for help when he and Eric found Jerome unconscious on the trail. Tommy wasn't part of the gang anymore; his friendship was only one of many losses Jerome had suffered since the last time he'd been in this place.

The young men got out of the car and started the half-mile trek from the ranger station to the sycamore. The trails were deserted. Eric and Jerome noted that the scene had changed with the season—no more green leaves blending with autumn foliage, just stark gray trunks amid occasional evergreens. No warm sun filtered through the tree limbs like it did that afternoon, only dreary fog and mist.

The foursome continued walking in silence. No one wanted to disturb Jerome.

Together they approached the accident site. Their steps were slow, cautious, almost as though they were walking on holy ground.

So this is it? This is where my so-called former life ended? Jerome stood in front of the tree that nearly killed him. He was surprised by the complete absence of anything special about the place. It was just a tree and trail like thousands of other trees and miles of other trails.

"You okay, dude?" Eric asked, breaking their silence.

Jerome turned and looked at the three faces before him: Eric. Steve. Matt. One good friend from his old life; two good friends from the new. Without this place, he'd have never met Matt, the physical therapist who understood him so well; he would never have bothered with Steve, whom he once dismissed as "Stevie stat boy." His friendship with Eric wouldn't have grown the way it had in the last several weeks. He understood his long-time friend now in ways he couldn't have before. Some things can only be learned through suffering, he realized, and now the two friends had a kind of suffering in common.

Yes, the friendships he had now, these new friendships, were a gift of his new life, a life he received at this very spot on the trail. And yes, he still had a life—he knew that now—a different life perhaps, but a good one. The losses he sustained as a result of his injury contained hidden gifts, gifts he was only just beginning to discover.

"Yeah. I'm okay," he replied, looking at his trusted friends. This place had no hold over him. It was time to move on. "Anybody up for another round of pizza?"

HOW TO PREVENT TBI

- Always wear a helmet when biking or riding a motorcycle or ATV.
- Always wear a helmet when using roller skates, riding a skateboard, skiing, playing ice hockey, horseback riding, or participating in other helmet-appropriate sports.
- Wear appropriate head gear for contact sports (boxing, football, lacrosse, etc.).
- Wear a seatbelt every time you drive or ride in a car.
- Never use alcohol or drugs when you drive.
- Play only on playgrounds where surfaces are made of shock-absorbing material (wood chips, mulch, sand, etc.).
- Avoid physical violence and guns.

To avoid brain injuries, always wear a helmet when riding a bike.

The water offers a good way to rebuild muscles after a brain injury. Despite the challenges they face, individuals with brain injuries can have lives that are both productive and full of joy.

TEN TIPS FOR COPING WITH TBI HEADACHES

Headaches can be a long-term consequence of a TBI. These tips might help reduce the frequency and severity of your headaches.

1. Try relaxation techniques (deep breathing, visualization, meditation, etc.).
2. Wear loose, comfortable clothing.
3. Get enough sleep.
4. Try to stick to a regular sleep schedule.
5. Try low-impact exercise (walking, swimming, etc.).
6. Avoid bright or fluorescent lighting.
7. Wear sunglasses in bright sunlight.
8. Note if certain foods seem to trigger a headache, and then eliminate those foods from your diet.
9. See your doctor. He may be able to prescribe medications or may recommend over-the-counter or herbal remedies known to provide relief.
10. Take approved or prescribed medications at the first sign of a headache.

QUOTES FROM SURVIVORS

"Never give up, always have hope, be patient, and take needed baby steps to get closer to your dreams and goals. Above all else, don't be your own worst enemy. Love who you are—brain injury and all."
—Jackie, victim of the 1985 terrorist hijacking of Egypt Air Flight 648, who was shot in the head and thrown from the plane to the tarmac. Today, Jackie runs her own business and is the author of *Miles to Go Before I Sleep* (Hazelden Publishing, 1996).

"If I were asked, I would counsel someone with a devastating injury not to focus on their loss and what might have been, but to fully live the life they have now and to carve out new and achievable dreams to fit it.

"This new life is truly mine. I own it and I am earnestly trying to learn . . . what God intends me to do with it.

"I was a happy woman before my injury, I am a happy one today."

—Dr. Claudia L. Osborn, who suffered a TBI when she was hit by a car while bicycling. Though unable to practice medicine because of her injury, she is a professor of internal medicine at Michigan State University.

FURTHER READING

Aaseng, Nathan, and Jay Aaseng. *Head Injuries.* New York: Franklin Watts-Grolier, 1996.

Hyde, Margaret O., and John F. Setaro. *When the Brain Dies First.* New York: Franklin Watts-Grolier, 2000.

Osborn, Claudia L. *Over My Head: A Doctor's Own Story of Head Injury from the Inside Looking Out.* Kansas City: Andrews McMeel Publishing, 1998, 2000.

Schoenbrodt, Lisa, ed. *Children with Traumatic Brain Injury: A Parents' Guide.* Bethesda, Md.: Woodbine House, 2001.

Stoler, Diane Roberts, and Barbara Albers Hill. *Coping with Mild Traumatic Brain Injury: A Guide to Living with the Problems Associated with Concussion/Brain Injury.* New York: Avery, 1998.

Swanson, Kara L. *I'll Carry the Fork!: Recovering a Life After Brain Injury.* Scotts Valley, Calif.: Rising Star Press, 1999, 2003.

FOR MORE INFORMATION

Brain Injury Association of America
105 North Alfred Street
Alexandria, VA 22314
(703) 236-6000
National Help Line: (800) 444-6443
publicrelations@biausa.org
www.biausa.org

Brain Injury.com
www.braininjury.com

Brave Kids
www.bravekids.org

Canadian Mental Health Association
8 King Street East, Suite 810
Toronto, ON, Canada M5C 1B5
(416) 484-7750
www.cmha.ca

Center for Neuro Skills
www.neuroskills.com

Head Injury Hotline & Brain Injury Resource Center
212 Pioneer Bldg
Seattle, WA 98104-2221
(206) 621-8558
www.headinjury.com

International Brain Injury Association
505 Wythe Street
Alexandria, VA 22314
(703) 683-8400
www.internationalbrain.org

National Center for Injury Prevention and Control
Mailstop F41, 4770 Buford Highway NE
Atlanta, GA 30341-3724
(770) 488-4031
www.cdc.gov/ncipc/tbi/default.htm

National Information Center for Children and Youth with Disabilities
P.O. Box 1492
Washington, DC 20013
(800) 695-0285 (v/TTY, for people using adaptive equipment)
www.nichcy.org

National Institute of Mental Health
NIMH Public Inquiries
6001 Executive Blvd., Room 8184, MSC 9663
Bethesda, MD 20892-9663
(301) 443-4513
www.nimh.nih.gov

The National Institute of Neurological Disorders and Stroke
NIH Neurological Institute
P.O. Box 5801
Bethesda, MD 20824
(800) 352-9424 or 301-496-5751 (voice)
(301) 468-5981 (TTY)
www.ninds.nih.gov/index.htm

National Rehabilitation Information Center (NARIC)
4200 Forbes Boulevard , Suite 202
Lanham, MD 20706-4829
(301) 562-2400; (800) 346-2742
www.naric.com

National Stroke Association
9707 East Easter Lane
Englewood, CO 80112-3747
(303) 649-9299; (800) STROKES (787-6537)
www.stroke.org

New York On-line Access to Health
www.noah-health.org/en/bns

Traumatic Brain Injury Survival
Dr. Glen Johnson, Clinical Neuropsychologist
Clinical Director of the Neuro-Recovery Head Injury Program
5123 North Royal Drive
Traverse City, MI 49684
(231) 935-0388
www.tbiguide.com

Traumatic Brain Injury Survival Guide (a free, downloadable on-line
    book)
www.tbiguide.com

The Waiting Room (for those who have a loved one in a coma)
www.waiting.com

Publisher's Note:

The Web sites listed on these pages were active at the time of publication.
The publisher is not responsible for Web sites that have changed their address or discontinued operation since the date of publication. The publisher will review and update the Web sites upon each reprint.

GLOSSARY

acceleration/deceleration injury: An injury where the head moves forward and comes to a sudden stop when it hits a non-moving object. Though the head stops, the brain moves until it collides with the front of the skull, injuring the brain's frontal lobe.

acquired brain injury: When the brain is damaged by strokes, tumors, lack of oxygen, poisons, near drowning, degenerative diseases, and other non-traumatic causes.

activities of daily living (ADLs): Feeding, grooming, dressing, bathing, writing, using a keyboard or telephone, etc.

ankle-foot orthosis (AFO): A molded plastic ankle brace. Also called a MAFO.

anoxia: Lack of oxygen to the brain.

cerebrospinal fluid (CSF): Fluid found in the brain cavity and spinal column.

closed-head injury: An injury to the head that does not penetrate the skull. These might include skull fracture, external bruises, and cuts on the face or scalp.

coma: A state of unconsciousness caused by illness or injury.

compensatory strategies: Alternate ways of accomplishing a task.

computed tomography or CT scans (also CAT scans): Tests like an X-ray that take cross-sectional images of the body that can detect bleeding, swelling, tumors, and other soft tissue injuries.

concussion: A minor brain injury that occurs when the brain collides with the skull.

congenital nervous injuries: Central nervous system injuries present at or before birth.

contusion: The bruising of a distinct area of brain tissue.

coup/contra-coup: An injury that occurs when a moving object hits the head, pressing the skull inward and causing the brain to strike the opposite side of the skull. Bruising occurs at two places: the part of the brain where the head was initially hit and the part of the brain that collided with the opposite side of the skull.

CPR: Cardiopulmonary resuscitation; a procedure to restore normal breathing that includes clearing the air passages, mouth-to-mouth respiration, and heart massage by pressing on the chest.

depressed skull fracture: When the skull cracks or breaks and pieces of the broken skull press into brain tissue.

diffuse brain injury: Tearing and stretching of microscopic connections throughout the brain; not limited to a specific or confined area.

diplegia: Partial or complete paralysis affecting both legs.

dura: Also, dura mater. The thick, outermost membrane between the skull and brain.

edema: Swelling in the brain, due to an accumulation of fluid in brain tissue.

epidural hematoma: Bleeding between the skull and dura mater.

fine motor skills: Abilities requiring the use of the body's smaller muscles, primarily in the hands.

Glasgow Coma Scale (GCS): A tool doctors use to determine the severity of a coma state.

gross motor skills: Abilities requiring the use of the body's larger muscles, like walking, sitting, and running.

hematoma: Bleeding in or around the brain.

hemiparesis: Muscle weakness on one side of the body.

hemiplegia: Partial or complete paralysis on one side of the body.

individualized education plan (IEP): An educational program designed for an individual student with special needs.

intracerebral hematoma: Bleeding within the brain.

magnetic resonance imaging (MRI): A medical test using magnetic fields to show greater detail than X-rays or CT scans.

multidisciplinary team: The group of professionals following a patient's recovery or a student's educational program. Jerome's team included the patient, the patient's parents, and several health-care professionals and therapists.

neurologist: A physician who specializes in the nervous system and its disorders.

occupational therapies: Rehab strategies designed to help patients improve their fine motor skills and become more independent with activities of daily living.

open-head injury: An injury occurring when an object pokes through the skull and dura, causing a specific, localized injury to the brain.

These include gunshot wounds, stabbings, or other injuries in which the head is opened or pierced by a foreign object.

paralysis: Loss of function or sensation in a part of the body; can be partial or complete.

paraplegia: Paralysis of the lower limbs and lower half of the body.

PDA: Personal digital (or data) assistant; a hand-held computer.

penetrating-head injury: An open-head injury.

penetrating-skull fracture: A skull fracture that penetrates brain tissue.

physical therapies: Rehab strategies designed to help the patient increase large muscle function and mobility.

post-concussive syndrome (PCS): A group of symptoms including but not limited to headaches, dizziness, memory loss, short-term memory problems, inability to concentrate, and emotional changes that persist after a concussion or head injury.

post-traumatic amnesia (PTA): The inability to recall events immediately surrounding a traumatic injury.

quadriplegia: Partial or complete paralysis of the entire body and all four limbs (both arms and both legs).

special education: Programs available in the public schools through which students with special needs can be identified and have their educational needs met.

subdural hematoma: Bleeding beneath the dura mater, between it and other membranes.

traumatic brain injury (TBI): Brain damage caused by an external force or blow to the head, as in automobile accidents, industrial accidents, falls, sports injuries, electric shock, physical abuse, whiplash, weapons injuries, acts of violence, and shaken-baby syndrome. TBIs can happen in both closed-head and open-head injuries.

ventilator: A device that artificially maintains breathing.

INDEX

BIOGRAPHIES

Joan Esherick is a full-time author, freelance writer, and professional speaker who lives outside of Philadelphia, Pennsylvania, with her husband and three teenagers, one of whom has had a brain injury since birth. Her recent books include *Our Mighty Fortress: Finding Refuge in God* (Moody Press, 2002), and multiple books with Mason Crest Publishers in their PSYCHIATRIC DISORDERS: DRUGS AND PSYCHOLOGY FOR THE MIND AND BODY series and in their YOUTH WITH SPECIAL NEEDS series. She has contributed dozens of articles to national periodicals and speaks nationwide.

Dr. Lisa Albers is a developmental behavioral pediatrician at Children's Hospital Boston and Harvard Medical School, where her responsibilities include outpatient pediatric teaching and patient care in the Developmental Medicine Center. She currently is Director of the Adoption Program, Director of Fellowships in Developmental and Behavioral Pediatrics, and collaborates in a consultation program for community health centers. She is also the school consultant for the Walker School, a residential school for children in the state foster-care system.

Dr. Carolyn Bridgemohan is an instructor in pediatrics at Harvard Medical School and is a board-certified developmental behavioral pediatrician on staff in the Developmental Medicine Center at Children's Hospital, Boston. Her clinical practice includes children and youth with autism, hearing impairment, developmental language disorders, global delays, mental retardation, and attention and learning disorders. Dr. Bridgemohan is coeditor of *Bright Futures Case Studies for Primary Care Clinicians: Child Development and Behavior*, a curriculum used nationwide in pediatric residency training programs.

Cindy Croft is the State Special Needs Director in Minnesota, coordinating Project EXCEPTIONAL MN, through Concordia University. Project EXCEPTIONAL MN is a state project that supports the inclusion of children in community settings through training, on-site consultation, and professional development. She also teaches as adjunct faculty for Concordia University, St. Paul, Minnesota. She has worked in the special needs arena for the past fifteen years.

Dr. Laurie Glader is a developmental pediatrician at Children's Hospital in Boston where she directs the Cerebral Palsy Program and is a staff pediatrician with the Coordinated Care Services, a program designed to meet the needs of children with special health-care needs. Dr. Glader also teaches regularly at Harvard Medical School. Her work with public agencies includes New England SERVE, an organization that builds connections between state health departments, health-care organizations, community providers, and families. She is also the staff physician at the Cotting School, a school specializing in the education of children with a wide range of special health-care needs.